A Passion for JESUS

A Passion for JUSTICE

ESTHER BYLE BRULAND
STEPHEN CHARLES MOTT

Judson Press® Valley Forge

Contents

Preface

Many Christians desire to expand and deepen their service for Christ but feel overwhelmed as they face the crying, complex needs of a burdened world. Many Christians are sure that their faith has relevance outside the doors of their church and home but have never had the chance to study, discuss, and apply the social implications of the gospel.

This workbook arose out of a desire on the part of the authors to respond to the needs of such Christians. To our knowledge, there existed no study book for lay people that would help them work through a biblical theology of Christian social responsibility and at the same time equip and enable them to respond to God's call to be people of justice and reconciliation. We set to work to fill that gap by creating this workbook.

We believe that this book might be useful in several settings. It could be used, for instance, as curriculum for an adult church school class, as study material for a Bible study group that desires more focus and outreach, as a guide for a newly constituted social-concerns committee in a church, or as a study book for an existing social-concerns committee that desires a renewed sense of vision and direction.

The substantive theological and ethical content of the narrative sections of the workbook has been adapted for a lay readership from materials prepared by Stephen Mott for training Christian leaders at the seminary level. The greater portion of those materials has recently been published by Oxford University Press under the title *Biblical Ethics and Social Change* (New York, 1982). The authors recommend this book to readers and study leaders who wish to delve further into any of the areas presented in this workbook or who desire to deepen their understanding of the theology and forms of Christian social involvement.

Introduction

The hollow eyes of the starving child stare out at us from the news photo in the morning paper. Sitting at the table, coffee in hand, we are moved. Our automatic reaction is to want to help that child. We look around. We have well-stocked cupboards, and we have the will to share. So why not do something?

But what? Can we really help? Our enthusiasm starts to wane. Somehow it just seems hopeless. There are so many problems in the world, and they are all so large and complex. The child's face flows into images of run-down, rat-infested tenements, . . . into scenes of violent crime against the elderly, . . . into pictures of long lines of unemployed workers. So much suffering.

We want to respond. We want to help, but we grow paralyzed at the magnitude of the problems. They make us feel small and helpless. And besides, we have personal responsibilities of our own to cope with. We turn the page to another section of the newspaper.

Where is God in this scenario? What does God's word tell us about human suffering and oppression and our role in relieving them? How can we take our faith outside the doors of the church so that it really is light and salt to a dark and decaying world?

This workbook addresses itself to these questions. Chapters 1 through 5 look at the causes of suffering and oppression; they focus on God's grace, love, and justice, which motivate us to respond to suffering and oppression and which enable us to do so; and they explore the nature of God's reign, which gives us the power with which to act, a standard toward which to aim, and a context within which to work. Chapters 6 through 11 look at various ways in which we can give hands and feet to our faith. Chapter 12 draws us to consider how to avoid or overcome pitfalls and strains that we may encounter as we serve.

Still, all the insights offered in this book will be of little use to us in bringing any real, lasting life and relief to a suffering world unless we first have a passion for Jesus. He made us; he gave his life for us; he is our king eternal. We are called to love him with all our heart, strength, and mind. We are called to commit our lives to him and to live according to his will as he has revealed it in his Word and through his Spirit. He gives us new life, he gives us new vision, and he gives us power to live as he has called us to live.

It is the premise of this book that a passion for Jesus leads his followers to have a passion for justice, a passion to work for the well-being of all other humans as we embody Christ's love to them. For we are Christ's body in the world, called and empowered by his Spirit to continue the task begun by Christ to "preach good news to the poor . . . to proclaim freedom for the prisoners and recovery of sight for the blind, to release the oppressed, to proclaim the year of the Lord's favor" (Luke 4:18-19).

Format and Use of the Workbook

Each chapter of this workbook consists of two basic parts: a narrative section and an "Engage" section. The narrative section sets forth biblical and theological background and foundations for Christian response to suffering and injustice. The "Engage" section consists of exercises designed to promote interaction with the material covered in the narrative content, to provide additional insight, and to help the reader move toward applying what he or she has learned.

This workbook lends itself to both individual and group use. The ideal usage would be for a group to commit itself to working through the material chapter by chapter. Individual group members would then read through the narrative section and do the exercises in the "Engage" section on their own. (It would be helpful to record answers to exercises from the "Engage" sections in a notebook to aid you in later reflection. Your notebook could also serve as a journal in which to chronicle your experiences and insights.) Then the members would come to the group meetings prepared to discuss the exercises and any questions or issues raised by the narrative section. A group setting for study of the material encourages interaction and the sharing of ideas, and it functions as a support structure for group members as they embark upon action.

Only insofar as you knowingly open yourself up to this workbook—listen to it; think about what you read; talk back to it, to yourself, and to your group; and act upon what you learn and discover—can it have an effect upon you that will help you to have an effect upon your world.

1

Battling Evil in Our World

The rumour of war grew behind them. Now they could hear, borne over the dark, the sound of harsh singing. They had climbed far up into the Deeping Coomb when they looked back. Then they saw torches, countless points of fiery light upon the black fields behind, scattered like red flowers, or winding up from the lowlands in long flickering lines. Here and there a larger blaze leapt up.

'It is a great host and follows us hard.' said Aragorn.

'They bring fire,' said Théoden, 'and they are burning as they come, rick, cot, and tree. This was a rich vale and had many homesteads. Alas for my folk!'

'Would that day was here and we might ride down upon them like a storm out of the mountains!' said Aragorn. 'It grieves me to fly before them.'

'We need not fly much further,' said Éomer. 'Not far ahead now lies Helm's Dike, an ancient trench and rampart scored across the coomb, two furlongs below Helm's Gate. There we can turn and give battle.'[1]

The forces of evil in struggle with the forces of good. We can see the struggle clearly here. Through the eyes of Aragorn, Théoden, and Éomer we watch the enemy advance, destroying the homes and lives of innocent people. With what righteous indignation they longed to stop this creeping evil! Yet the darkness and their position impeded them. Not willing to let their dastardly foe win out, they continued their retreat, seeking a more strategic position from which to give battle.

The struggle between good and evil is not always so clear to us as it is in this battle scenario. Yet the struggle constantly goes on. It is the reality behind the reality that we see. The apostle Paul makes this clear in his letter to the Ephesians.

Finally, be strong in the Lord and in his mighty power. Put on the full armor of God so that you can take your stand against the devil's schemes.

> For our struggle is not against flesh and blood, but against the rulers, against the authorities, against the powers of this dark world and against the spiritual forces of evil in the heavenly realms. Therefore put on the full armor of God, so that when the day of evil comes, you may be able to stand your ground, and after you have done everything, to stand (Ephesians 6:10-13).

Satan and his evil forces are prowling the world, struggling for control over God's creation. He wages battle on many fronts.

We have all felt the battle within us. Paul expressed it aptly in Romans 7:21-25.

> So I find this law at work: When I want to do good, evil is right there with me. For in my inner being I delight in God's law; but I see another law at work in the members of my body, waging war against the law of my mind and making me a prisoner of the law of sin at work within my members. What a wretched man I am! Who will rescue me from this body of death? Thanks be to God—through Jesus Christ our Lord!

Paul knew that Christ had conquered the powers of evil in his sacrificial death and victorious resurrection. Paul knew what it was to live in the power of this victory. But Paul also knew that he would continually have to struggle with the forces of evil as long as he lived on this earth. He could not and would not settle into lethargy. Christ's reign must be proclaimed!

We also face this battle in the area of our relationships. The family, in particular, is a constant battleground for the forces of good and evil. While many of a person's happiest experiences take place in the context of the family, it can also be the source of one's deepest hurts and anxieties.

> . . . We find that most experts tell us that even in the most stable of families, one still finds power struggles, rivalries, sulking, quarreling, and complaining. In relation to the other family members, it is not unusual for people to feel jealous, guilty, anxious, or frustrated . . . Why do one-third of marriages end in divorce in the U.S. today? . . . Why is there increasing concern about the "battered child syndrome?" Why are one-fourth of all murders committed within a family?[2]

Why? Because the forces of evil continue to struggle for control of this arena. It is no wonder that so many church sermons, so many books, and so many articles by Christians today are aimed at strengthening family life.

However, the battle is not confined to the family but proliferates wherever there are interpersonal relationships. At work, at school, in the long line at the grocery store, in darkened barrooms, and in well-lit offices. The mysterious power of evil sinks root and tries to grow. We must battle it in ourselves. We must battle it in our relationships. Satan's forces long to conquer yet another area of our human life. They long to infiltrate, permeate, and dominate at the level of our larger, more complex social relationships. Much power resides at this level, in our institutions and social structures. We have handed a good deal of control over our lives to our local, state, and national governments; to corporations; to schools; to banks; to agencies; to public utilities; and to special interests. Can we trust those in charge to act morally and ethically, not only in their personal lives, not only in their interpersonal relationships, but also in their complicated decisions that will affect large numbers of people? By what criteria do they make those decisions and in favor of whom? Are they held accountable for how they dispense the power granted them? By whom?

Many of the social structures to which we grant power take the form of a bureaucracy. Because it is stable and orderly, a bureaucracy is basically an efficient way of getting things done, despite a reputation for spewing out red tape. Everyone has a job to do and is granted the power to do that job. Responsibility is spread out among all the individuals employed in a bureaucracy; no one person holds ultimate and overriding power.

Yet because of the diffuse nature of its organization, a bureaucratic system easily lends itself to the inroads of evil. Generally no one has or takes complete responsibility for any decision. It is an unusual bureaucrat who goes beyond the confines of his or her delegated task to make sure that the entire task is carried out as designated. And rarely, if ever, does anyone monitor the outcome of the entire task to see if it achieves what was intended or serves the broader purposes of society. Frequently, bureaucracies end up serving largely their own vested interests. There is nothing inherently wrong with bureaucracies or any other social structures. They perform much good in society, and they even prevent certain evils. Yet because they are made up of individuals and, even more so, because they have a life of their own that extends beyond the individuals of which they are composed, they suffer an unending siege from the forces of evil.

This evil takes hold on several levels.

- A white-collar executive "plays the system" and, unnoticed by anyone, embezzles hundreds of dollars each month.

- A man works for the gas company. The nature of the job and of his skills force him to travel in the field away from his family. His absence becomes a pivotal factor in the break-up of the family. The job requires his absence from home and no one can point to a certain person who made the job that way.

● The staff of an office of a federal agency orders thousands of dollars worth of office equipment and supplies that they will never use because they fear that if they don't use up their allotted budget, they will not receive the same or an increased allotment in the next year's budget. At the same time, programs to help the poor are being cut because of a lack of federal monies.

● A public utility which supplies natural gas to a large Eastern city makes a mistake in ordering fuel for the approaching winter. Knowing there will be a shortage, they try covering up the mistake rather than notifying the public and taking proper rectifying measures. Near-crisis conditions occur.

● Despite protests and public outrage, a large corporation persists in marketing an infant formula in Africa, which has led to the deaths of many infants. Their false and flashy advertising lures many un-knowing mothers into buying the formula.

● Under the principles of "economic development," multinational corporations disrupt and destroy the economies of many third world countries by bleeding them for more assets than the corporations initially invested, as well as by destroying the native businesses which originally existed.

How can this evil be stopped? Developing moral and ethical respon-sibility in individuals is important and can make a difference. Yet it is not enough. As we saw before, social structures have a life of their own. While the individuals who make them up come and go, social institutions maintain a continuous existence. Policies may come to have more importance than those who created them and those who enforce them. We face here not individual evil but structural evil, which often goes unnoticed because it is diffused throughout large, complex systems. We are aware of the negative effects that this evil produces, but we tend to have no more than a vague awareness of its actual presence and operation within our social systems. It is vital that we be as sharp in discerning social evil as we are, or should be, in discerning personal evil.

We must wage the battle against evil in the locations in which we find it, and with the appropriate strategy. Evil in the individual heart must be confronted there and called to repentance and renewal. Structural evils that prey upon individuals and upon peoples must be seen as such and confronted on the structural level by Christians bonded together in the task of overcoming the oppressor and aiding the oppressed. Christ's reign must be proclaimed!

ENGAGE

Where Should We Focus Our Energies?

Most Christians would agree that we are clearly commanded to confront evil in our personal lives and relationships. We face this responsibility perhaps most dramatically at the time of our own conversion. We see our own evil nature confronted with the fact of God's holiness. We sense the Spirit's call to accept Christ's sacrifice on our behalf. We respond, repenting of our evil, and we taste Christ's victory as he washes away our sinfulness and makes new creatures out of us.

It is part of our nature as new creatures, modeled after Christ, to hate evil and to want to see it obliterated wherever it lurks. We want other people to feel the burden of their evil natures lifted; so we share our experience and Christ's love with them. We encourage them to respond to his call to repentance and renewal. We are urged in the Bible and from the pulpit to purge ourselves of evil thoughts, intents, and practices and to live according to an ethic of love and justice.

It is pretty easy to see how this ethic should be played out on the personal level—easier, indeed, to see it than to do it. But when we see evil operating at the social level, we are plagued by questions, doubts, and uneasiness. Social systems are so complex, could my concern and desire to confront evil here make any difference? Even if I chose a manageable problem and a workable strategy, could I make even a dent in an existing social problem? Wouldn't God rather I spend my time working with individuals, helping them to see their need for repentance?

God is *very much* concerned with individuals. But something we frequently miss in our reading of Scripture and something we infrequently hear preached from the pulpit is that God is also *very much* concerned about the social order. God hates social evil and the suffering it causes. We have a tendency, in setting our agenda as Christians and as a church, to order priorities *for* God, according to what is most appealing and least threatening for us. But God calls us to a deeper faith, a broader concern, and a higher obedience.

Let's take a look in the Bible at an example of God's concern about social evil and suffering, and God's calling of a servant to obey God and address the problem.

The Context

Read Exodus 1:1-16; then answer the following questions:
1. Who was oppressing the people of Israel? (vv.8-10)

2. What motivated the oppression? (vv.9-10)

3. How were they oppressed? (vv.11-16)

4. Can you see God's hand at work in this passage, acting to preserve Israel? (vv.7,12)

The Call and Commission of Moses

Read Exodus 2:23-3:12; then answer the following questions:
1. What evidences do we have of God's concern about the evil oppression of Israel? (2:23-25, 3:7-9)

2. To what action was God moved as he contemplated Israel's oppressed condition? (3:7-8)

3. To what task did God call Moses? (3:10)

4. By what authority was Moses to go to Pharaoh to claim Israel's liberation? (3:11-12)

Chapters 5 through 12 of Exodus report the dramatic and miraculous events that led up to the actual liberation of Israel from its oppressors. Let us continue, however, to contemplate God's initial commissioning of Moses to lead in this liberation.

Considering the Implications

1. What made Egypt's oppression of Israel a *social* rather than a personal evil?

   (Hints: Look at the nature and number of the oppressors, and the type of power they held; look at who was oppressed; look at the nature and breadth of the oppression; look at the results of the oppression.)

2. What makes God's call to Moses, telling him to go to the pharaoh, a form of social action?

3. Consider how different things would have been if God had been concerned *only* with individual evil and individual action.

   (For example: Moses and the Israelites could have spent years trying to evangelize their oppressors. If they had succeeded in converting individual Egyptians, they would still have had to face the problem of an oppressive government and social system. They would still have been wrongly enslaved and suffering.)

4. What motivated God to liberate Israel from social oppression?

5. What motivated Moses to obey God and engage in social action on behalf of Israel?

6. Do you think God's concern with social evil and suffering is limited to the Old Testament times?

What Might God Commission You to Do If You Were to Meet God Today at a Burning Bush?

Think about that. Think about your world—your life, your neighborhood concerns, your community, your workplace, places you do business, your involvement in local, state, and national government, concerns you read about in the newspapers, etc. Where do you see social evil at work in your world, pervading and perverting, struggling to outdo the forces of good?* Where does God see suffering and bondage?

Try to put yourself in Moses' place at the burning bush. What evil might God call you to address in your own world? It need not be of grandiose proportions, though it might be. What evil and suffering would God see in your world? What might God call you, as God's agent, to do in God's power? (Record your thoughts so you can refer to them later.)

What Can Be Done?

In the last paragraph of the narrative portion of this chapter, I wrote that "we must wage the battle against evil in the locations in which

*Beware! It is easy to see only good in the social systems that favor one's own interests. Scrutinize these as carefully and critically as you do those systems that do not favor your interests.

we find it, and with the appropriate strategy.'' Let's deal with this in more detail now.

We have seen that evil has a varied geography. It is found in a range of locations—from the human hearts to the most complex social institution. Our strategies for combatting evil must correspond to the range of locations in which we find it. Evangelism and Christian nurture address evil in the individual heart—bringing a person to a saving faith in Jesus Christ, and discipling him or her into the victorious and holy life of Christ's reign.

When it comes to addressing social evil, there are four basic levels at which people can respond.

1. *Personal action.* This is basically what people refer to as social service, or simply as "helping out." It is a socially responsive, caring ministry that takes place between individuals; for example, when an orphan child is adopted, or when needy people are counseled, visited, supplied with resources, or aided with transportation.

2. *Personal involvement in institutions.* This response involves personal ministries of social concern which are carried out through contacts in an institutional setting. Examples would be visiting a nursing home, prison, or hospital and volunteering in a tutoring program or referral ministry.

3. *Voluntary group action.* This involves creating or working with groups that have a purpose of social change or social care. Examples would be raising funds and gathering other resources to open a medical clinic in an area with few health care resources; opening and operating a rape crisis center; and creating a neighborhood organization to deal with common concerns.

4. *Structural/institutional action.* This action is directed at bringing about justice in the major institutions of our society. It addresses the institutions and activities of government, business, education, finance, and so forth. Examples of such action would be lobbying to change a law, working to reform public education, and boycotting a specific manufacturer to protest certain of its policies and practices.

The level at which a person chooses to respond depends on the nature of the problem to be addressed; the person's gifts, skills, and resources; his or her vision for what changes might be brought about and how; and the presence or absence of other people with whom to work for change. One essential element of each form of action is the need for prayer. We are involved in spiritual warfare. As servants of the Lord Jesus Christ, we must be in constant communion with him, seeking his perfect will and his perfect power in our lives and in our world.

One person cannot cure the ills of the world, but one person can make a big difference. Where would Israel have been if Moses had decided not to leave his sheep? Yet even Moses didn't go it alone. He had the support of Aaron and Miriam, and later on he shared his task of leadership with several other judges. Most importantly, he had a vision given him from God, a clear understanding of the causes of Israel's oppression, a sense of God's justice and a grasp of God's promise to Israel, and a willingness to take some active responsibility in confronting Pharaoh and leading Israel.

Let us, like Moses, be open to God's summons to confront social evil. We must be aware of our strengths, doing as much as we can with the abilities, resources, and vision that God has given us. And when we face limitations, let us give whatever support we can to those who can do what we cannot.

2

Saved by Grace,
Moved by Grace

Enemy-occupied territory—that is what this world is. Christianity is the
story of how the rightful king has landed, you might say landed in disguise,
and is calling us all to take part in a great campaign of sabotage.[1]

O ur King has liberated us! Just as God felt compassion for the people
of Israel and liberated them from their oppression and bondage
in the land of Egypt, so God has felt compassion for us and has set us
free from the oppression and bondage of evil by a great work of grace.
Everything we are and everything we have, we owe to this grace.

In the Bible, we see God's grace portrayed as a great river of living
water. In the forty-seventh chapter of Ezekiel, the prophet reported a
vision that the Lord had given him of a river of water issuing forth
from the temple. The further the river progressed, the wider and deeper
it grew—like no ordinary river—until it could not be crossed. Fresh
and sweet, it brought forth abundant life.

"And wherever the river goes every living creature which swarms will
live, and there will be very many fish; for this water goes there, that the
waters of the sea may become fresh; so everything will live where the
river goes. . . . And on the banks, on both sides of the river, there will
grow all kinds of trees for food. Their leaves will not wither nor their fruit
fail, but they will bear fresh fruit every month, because the water for them
flows from the sanctuary. Their fruit will be for food, and their leaves for
healing" (Ezekiel 47:9-12, RSV).

In Ezekiel's vision this tremendous river brought life even to the
stagnant waters of the Dead Sea, which previously could support no
life. What a picture of the way God's saving grace flows forth abundantly, saving us from our death in sin, and creating new life in us!
Just as the fish and trees described by Ezekiel depended upon the river

for life and for fruitfulness, so we are dependent upon God's grace for our sustenance and empowerment to do God's good will.[2]

Jesus similarly portrayed God's saving grace as living water in his conversation with the Samaritan woman at the well. Referring to the well, Jesus said to her,

> "Everyone who drinks this water will be thirsty again, but whoever drinks the water I give him will never thirst. Indeed, the water I give him will become in him a spring of water welling up to eternal life" (John 4:13-14).

Jesus used the same imagery in reference to his Spirit, who embodies God's grace in us.

> "If [anyone thirsts], . . . come to me and drink. Whoever believes in me, as the Scripture has said, streams of living water will flow from within [that one]." By this he meant the Spirit, whom those who believed in him were later to receive (John 7:37-39).*

When we were withering away in our sin, God poured out abundant grace toward us through the sacrifice of God's own son. Jesus' death and resurrection made *life* possible. God's Spirit draws us to repent of our sins and to drink deeply of the life-giving, living water. We are filled to overflowing with God's grace.

God's Spirit continues to work in us and with us, to make us more like Christ. Though the world we live in still bears the taint of evil, the Spirit is constantly cleansing and renewing us so that we can live in this world as the new creatures that we have been made in Christ.

God's work in us and God's will for us do not stop at this point. God calls us to *live* by the power of grace, bringing forth fruit and letting the rivers of living water flow out of our hearts to bring life to others.

> For it is by grace you have been saved, through faith—and this not from yourselves, it is the gift of God—not by works, so that no one can boast. For we are God's workmanship, created in Christ Jesus to do good works, which God prepared in advance for us to do (Ephesians 2:8-10).

We were created and saved to do God's good works of grace on earth. God's grace flows abundantly toward us. We drink deeply of it, and its life-giving power produces lush growth in us, with a purpose. We are to be channels of God's grace to others in our human relationships.

*Material printed in brackets in some Scripture references in this book represents a translation by the authors which reflects the inclusive language used in the original Greek or Hebrew.

Like the trees sustained by the river which flowed from the temple, our fruit is to be for food and our leaves for healing.

The apostle Paul makes it clear that we must prune away some ugly, unfruitful branches if we are to be effective channels of God's grace.

Get rid of all bitterness, rage and anger, brawling and slander, along with every form of malice. Be kind and compassionate to one another, forgiving each other, just as in Christ God forgave you.

Be imitators of God, therefore, as dearly loved children and live a life of love, just as Christ loved us and gave himself up for us as a fragrant offering and sacrifice to God (Ephesians 4:31–5:2).

Our task consists of imitating our gracious God. We are to do in our circle of relationships what God does. Jesus told a parable to illustrate this and also to issue a warning to those who might refuse to be as gracious with others as God has been with them. Matthew 18:23-35 recounts the parable of a king who was settling accounts with his servants. One servant owed the king about ten million dollars. Because he could not pay the debt, the king was going to sell him and his family into slavery. The man pleaded for mercy, and out of pity for him the king graciously forgave him the entire debt. The servant then went out and ran into a man who owed him about twenty dollars. He grabbed him by the throat and demanded payment. When the man said he could not pay, the servant had him thrown into jail, despite the man's pleas for mercy. The king soon heard about this, and called the servant to him. "You wicked servant," he said, "I cancelled all that debt of yours because you begged me to. Shouldn't you have had mercy on your fellow servant just as I had on you?" Whereupon the king had his servant thrown into prison until he could pay his debt. Jesus summed up the parable with the warning, "This is how my heavenly Father will treat each of you unless you forgive your brother from your heart" (Matthew 18:32-35).

We are called to follow God's example. God wants us to be channels of the grace and mercy that God has poured forth toward us, not only in our personal interactions and relationships, but also in matters of social justice. This is not an either/or situation, *either* acting with grace toward individuals *or* mirroring God's grace toward social systems. It is a spectrum—of seeking the good of others, of living righteously, of acting justly and compassionately in all our personal and social relationships, and of prophetically calling for justice and good to be done in our social structures.

The Old Testament abounds with instructions for the people of Israel to deal justly in their social relationships, reflecting toward others the grace that God showed them in liberating them from their bondage in Egypt.

> Do not deprive the alien or the fatherless of justice, or take the cloak of the widow as a pledge. Remember that you were slaves in Egypt and the LORD your God redeemed you from there. That is why I command you to do this (Deuteronomy 24:17-18).

The "alien" (or stranger), "the fatherless," and "the widow" are not only terms that refer to literal strangers, orphans, and widows; they are also regional metaphors representing *anyone* who was poor and powerless.

The concern for the stranger is a recurring theme, based on the remembrance that the people of Israel were once strangers in the land of Egypt.[3] That Israel is frequently reminded to treat strangers with the same loving concern that they would show one of their own demonstrates to us that our responsibility is not limited solely to other believers. God's love and grace flow abundantly to all.

> For the LORD your God is God of gods and Lord of lords, the great God, mighty and awesome, who shows no partiality and accepts no bribes. He defends the cause of the fatherless and the widow, and loves the alien, giving him food and clothing. And you are to love those who are aliens, for you yourselves were aliens in Egypt (Deuteronomy 10:17-19).

Just as God called Israel to love the aliens and to care for them, we are to love and care for those outside of the church, as well as those within, because we were once aliens outside of Christ's body, and we are still aliens in a secular society.

> But you are a chosen people, a royal priesthood, a holy nation, a people belonging to God, that you may declare the praises of him who called you out of darkness into his wonderful light. Once you were not a people, but now you are the people of God; once you had not received mercy, but now you have received mercy.
> Dear friends, I urge you, as aliens and strangers in the world, to abstain from sinful desires, which war against your soul. Live such good lives among the pagans that, though they accuse you of doing wrong, they may see your good deeds and glorify God on the day he visits us (1 Peter 2:9-12).

We also see a tremendous concern for the poor in the instructions given to Israel before they went to inhabit the Promised Land. Again the people of Israel were called to allow God's rich grace to flow through them to others. They were not to pool up the benefits for themselves but were to be channels of the life that comes from God.

If there is a poor man among your brothers in any of the towns of the land that the LORD your God is giving you, do not be hardhearted or tightfisted toward your poor brother. Rather be openhanded and freely lend him whatever he needs (Deuteronomy 15:7-8).

When you are harvesting in your field and you overlook a sheaf, do not go back to get it. Leave it for the alien, the fatherless and the widow, so that the LORD your God may bless you in all the work of your hands. . . . When you harvest the grapes in your vineyard, do not go over the vines again. Leave what remains for the alien, the fatherless and the widow. Remember that you were slaves in Egypt. That is why I command you to do this (Deuteronomy 24:19-22).

These were some of the basic guidelines set down for a nation that was called to represent God on the earth! Israel was a "called-out people," God called them out to nurture them and teach them in a special way, so that they might demonstrate to the other peoples of the world what their creator was—a just God, a holy God, a mighty God, a compassionate God. God motivated Israel to do good by showing gracious love and good works toward them. They were called simply to glorify God, acting toward others as God had acted toward them. Like the river flowing from the temple, they were to bring life to all with whom they came in contact.

In the New Testament, as well, we see this call to compassion, motivated by the compassion of God's grace. In 2 Corinthians, chapters 8 and 9, Paul challenges the Corinthian Christians to let God's grace toward them find expression in their grace to the poor. Specifically, Paul was taking up an offering, a love gift for the poor Jewish Christians in Jerusalem. These people were persecuted economically, politically, and socially because of their profession of faith in Jesus Christ. As a result they were destitute. Paul set about to relieve their desperate condition by asking the churches in Macedonia to give what they could to help out these Jerusalem Christians. He wrote to the Christians in Corinth, reporting on his progress and requesting their participation.

Paul encouraged the Corinthians to join in the joy of sharing with their poorer brothers and sisters by telling them of the beautiful, generous response of their sister churches of Macedonia. He tied all this to the powerful motivation of acting toward others as Christ had so generously acted toward them.

For you know the grace of our Lord Jesus Christ, that though he was rich, yet for your sakes he became poor, so that you through his poverty might become rich. (2 Corinthians 8:9).

God's grace motivates us to respond to others in like manner, just as God has blessed us. It also provides us with the ability to respond. God supplies not only the will, but also the way.

> And God is able to make all grace abound to you, so that in all things at all times, having all that you need, you will abound in every good work (2 Corinthians 9:8).

To summarize, everything we are and everything we have, we owe to God's grace, which flows toward us and in us abundantly with its life-giving power. Because of God's gracious acts toward us, we are called—indeed we *desire*—to act graciously toward others. Because on the cross Christ took compassion on us in our poverty and bondage, we are to take compassion on the poverty of others, and to act as liberators. God's grace not only acts within us to motivate us to do these good works, but it also gives us the resources and ability to do them. We can exclaim with Paul, "Thanks be to God for his inexpressible gift!"

ENGAGE

How Grace Would Respond

It is one thing to have an idea in our minds of how God's grace works in our lives, of what it means to be motivated and empowered by this grace to do God's good works on earth. It is another thing to respond to God's grace in our lives and in our deeds. It is one thing to see how Israel and the New Testament Christians lived out the ethics of grace; it is another thing to live out these ethics in our own lives and times.

God's grace and ethics are timeless and unchanging; however, the situations in which we must live out God's grace change. The following minicases will give you practice in discerning how God would have us respond, with grace, to contemporary situations.

As you read each minicase, ask yourself the following questions. (Charts are provided for recording your answers to each case.)

1. What is the basic problem in this situation?

2. What are the structural causes of this problem? (That is, what are the causes which go beyond the personal decisions or responsibility of any one person or couple?)

3. What other causes do you see (causes which might be more personal or situation-specific)?

4. What are the consequences? (That is, how do these causes result in suffering?)

5. How would God's spirit in me move me to bring relief from the evil and suffering in this situation? (Remember to address both the cause and the effect as you answer this question. Also, you will no doubt experience a conflict between what you feel should be done and what you feel would be in your power to do. In such cases, answer the question both ways: This is what should be done. . . . This is what I feel I could do at this point. . . .)

For help in getting started, look at the first minicase, found at the end of this chapter on page 28, which I have completed as an example. After you have looked at that minicase, examine the ones on pages 29 and 30 before reading on.

It has most likely become clear to you that there is not always a pat and simple answer to every situation. Even when we can discover the general direction in which grace would move us, we may likely encounter forks in the road. There is not always one best way to respond. To the best of our ability we must discern which alternative will maximize the good results and minimize the bad results. In all of this, then, it is vital to be in close communion with God—in prayerful thanksgiving for God's grace, in a growing relationship with God's gracious Spirit, and in prayerful dedication of ourselves to living out the ethics of grace as God has revealed them to us.

> Therefore, my dear friends, as you have always obeyed—not only in my presence, but now much more in my absence—continue to work out your salvation with fear and trembling, for it is God who works in you to will and to act according to his good purpose (Philippians 2:12-13).

Grace at Work in Me

It is time to do some self-examination. We've taken a look at how God's grace might motivate and empower us to respond in three specific minicases. But what about the experience of grace in our own lives? Consider the following questions:

1. Are you aware of the work of God's Spirit in your life? as the One who led you to repent of your sinfulness and commit your life to Christ your Savior? as the One who constantly works in you to make you more and more like Christ in character and in action? as the One who moves you to do the good works of God in your daily life and gives you the power to do them?

2. Try to think of several specific acts which you have been motivated to do in the past out of your gratitude for God's graciousness toward you and in response to God's call to be likewise gracious to others.

3. What new opportunities for acting in grace toward others are you aware of now that you were not aware of before? (Not only in general, but specific opportunities for action in your own life which would aid persons, groups, and even social structures.)

More on Motivation

We have looked at length at the power of God's grace, motivating us and enabling us to do good works on earth. As Christians we are to embrace God's grace and yield to God's perfect way in our lives.

At the same time, as humans, we are never pure in our motivations. We operate on several levels, and we respond to various stimuli. While we recognize God's grace as a major factor working in our lives, we are also motivated by our own economic and social needs, by personality needs and strengths, by cultural factors, etc. The personal make-up and the life circumstances of people vary. In addition, God has given each of us a free will. So, while it is the same God and the same grace that work in us, our responses to stimuli vary as we make different choices with our free wills.

Speed Leas and Paul Kittlaus, in their book *The Pastoral Counselor in Social Action,* describe five types of people who may consider taking part in socially responsive, caring ministries.[4]

1. People who have so many problems of their own that they have no energy or resources left for anything other than the personal struggle for physical or emotional survival.

2. People who are "feeling a pinch," who "are hindered from full functioning and appreciation of life because of difficulties that stem from social or environmental causes." Because they "feel a pinch," these people are motivated to confront, through social action, the social or environmental causes of their difficulties.

3. People wanting to do more. People who are "aware that they have been given much, and are thankful for the abundance they have received. . . . Out of gratitude, out of a sense of what they have to share, they desire to give or to help."

4. People already involved in caring ministries, under the auspices

of the local church, affiliated with some community organization, etc.

5. People not ready to get involved, people who are not interested, who don't show up at meetings, who argue about almost every action idea proposed, and who say they will do a task but then fail to follow through.

Do you see yourself in any of these descriptions? How does the motivation of God's grace fit with the other motivating factors in your life?

Minicase 1: You are a few paces behind an elderly couple in an aisle of the grocery store. They are poorly but neatly dressed. You hear them trying to decide whether they should buy the groceries they need, or whether they should buy less than they need so they can pay their heating bill.

Basic problem:	The couple does not have the financial ability to meet their own basic needs.
Structural causes:	① An economic system that forces the elderly into retirement without ensuring adequate financial security. ② Spiraling inflation which strains fixed incomes. ③ Gov't policies that grant financial advantages to the rich at the expense of the poor. ④ Expensive food packaging & marketing practices which inflate prices.
Other causes:	This couple obviously lacks (or refuses) help from other outside sources, such as family, church, community organizations, etc.
Consequences:	This couple will suffer from either inadequate nutrition, inadequate heat, or both. This could contribute to premature death.
What should be done to bring relief:	① Offer them money. ② Ask if they are aware of the food & heat subsidy programs in town. ③ Ask permission to submit their names to the church deacon's fund and/or ecumenical relief fund. ④ Ask congressional representatives to support legislation which favors economic justice for the poor and elderly. ⑤ Join a consumer's lobbying group for fairer pricing.
What I feel I could do:	List here the numbers of the above measures which you feel you have the power to do right now . . .

Minicase 2: You and a person of another race are the only qualified applicants for a job that has a good salary. During your interview, the person in charge of hiring tells you, off the record, that while your credentials are not quite as good as those of the other applicant, you will be awarded the job because "The boss doesn't want any of *those* people working here!"

Basic problem:	
Structural causes:	
Other causes:	
Conse quences:	
What should be done to bring relief:	
What I feel I could do:	

Minicase 3: In the latest edition of your city's newspaper, you read the following headlines: "PRESIDENT ASKS CONGRESS TO RAISE DEFENSE BUDGET"; "WELFARE AND FOOD STAMP PROGRAMS WILL BE CUT DRASTICALLY SAYS CABINET OFFICIAL"; and "MANY MIDDLE AND UPPER INCOME FAMILIES WILL BENEFIT FROM FEDERAL TAX CUTS."

Basic problem:	
Structural causes:	
Other causes:	
Consequences:	
What should be done to bring relief:	
What I feel I could do:	

3

Love Has Hands and Feet

For the grace of God that brings salvation has appeared to all. . . .
Jesus Christ, who gave himself for us to redeem us from all wickedness
and to purify for himself a people that are his very own, eager to do what
is good (Titus 2:11-14).

There are mystery stories, and then there are *mystery* stories. A really
good mystery story captures your attention right away. Something
goes drastically wrong. Who is responsible? Why did it happen? Can
the truth be uncovered? Can things be made right? Clue after clue
appears. The suspense builds. No detail goes unnoticed; no event goes
unexamined as you try to piece all the clues together. Your mind races;
you lose track of time. You have one thing on your mind: the *answer*.
You want all the pieces to form a whole. Soon the mystery consumes
you so that you feel you will burst if you can't solve it.

When the answer finally comes, it brings relief. Relief from the
tension of not knowing. Relief because the answer sheds light on all
the details. And relief that everything *does* fit together into a meaningful
whole.

The Bible contains the best mystery I've ever read. Events unroll
quickly. No sooner, it seems, did God finish creating Adam and Eve
than they blew it by disobeying God in the garden. Evil took hold as
Adam and Eve ripped to shreds the beautiful, perfect relationship they
had with their Creator God. *Now* what would happen? Would God wash
God's hands of humankind? Would God's grace change course and
flow in some other direction, leaving human life a desert?

The plot thickens. Far from giving up on humankind, God continued
to reach out. In a very significant action, God chose Abraham and his
descendants to receive God's grace and represent God on earth. The

31

whole history of the people of Israel is one big clue to God's mysterious plan for rescuing fallen human beings.

Clue after clue emerges. Event after event sheds light on this unfurling mystery. Some of the biblical characters seemed to grasp what was going on. The sacrifices must be a clue. . . . The law points us in the right direction. . . . And those prophets! They almost gave it away!

Finally, in the fullness of time, God revealed the solution to the mystery, the living answer to how God's created beings might be made acceptable again to their Maker. Jesus Christ, God in the flesh. God sent God's grace into the world, possessing hands and feet. The answer to the mystery, and yet, what a mystery in itself!

Grace with hands and feet. Of course! How else could God's divine purpose be accomplished? Jesus, God's Son, had to enter the world in human form. By the example of his life, Jesus had to show human beings how their Maker would have them live. By the power of his death and resurrection, he had to rescue them from the power of evil and reestablish their communion with their Creator.

What a task Jesus had to perform! He had no doubts, however, as to how to go about it. He understood God's will. In his every word and deed, Jesus showed us that God's grace is most fully expressed through active love.

> One of them, an expert in the law, tested him with this question: "Teacher, which is the greatest commandment in the Law?"
> Jesus replied: "'Love the Lord your God with all your heart and with all your soul and with all your mind.' This is the first and greatest commandment. And the second is like it: 'Love your neighbor as yourself.' All the Law and the Prophets hang on these two commandments" (Matthew 22:37-40).

Jesus totally loved God, and he steadfastly showed God's love toward every human "neighbor." He gave us a living definition of the active love which God requires of us.

Describing his mission in action terms, Jesus quoted the following from the prophet Isaiah.

> "The Spirit of the Lord is on me,
>   because he has anointed me
>   to preach good news to the poor.
> He has sent me to proclaim freedom for the prisoners
>   and recovery of sight for the blind,
> to release the oppressed,
>   to proclaim the year of the Lord's favor."
>   —Luke 4:18-19

Jesus lived out God's love by literally fulfilling these words in his life.

He preached the Good News, showing his compassion for the poor, the captives, the blind, and the oppressed. He loved with his hands and his feet.

Jesus' feet carried him on preaching tours throughout Palestine, step after step after step, along hot, dusty roads. His feet did not stop until he had reached the place of need. Jesus' hands ministered to the needs of others. They opened the eyes of the blind and lifted the lame to their feet. They broke bread, blessed it, and passed it to the hungry. And they pointed the way to the Father.

Jesus' hands and feet entered into his supreme act of love, receiving the nails that held him to the cross. Showing the ends to which God's love will go, Jesus laid down his life so that through his death and resurrection we might be given the power to live and love.

We who are members of Christ's body are called to be his hands and feet on earth today. We have quite a task before us if we are to love others as he has loved us.

> This is how we know what love is: Jesus Christ laid down his life for us. And we ought to lay down our lives for our brothers. If anyone has material possessions and sees his brother in need but has no pity on him, how can the love of God be in him? Dear children, let us not love with words or tongue but with actions and in truth (1 John 3:16-18).

Through our words and our deeds, we are to follow Christ's example of active love. We are to lay down our own selfish desires so that Christ's love within us may freely reach out to meet the needs of others.

Jesus made it clear that our love must extend to all persons, not just to those that we find lovely (Matthew 5:43-48). He went even further in revealing to us the quality of love that God expects from us. We must show Godlike love not only in our behavior toward others, but also in our intent (Matthew 5:21-22). This love that is our duty as members of Christ's body is described to us in terms of the two strongest forces we know: God's love for us in Christ, and our love for ourselves. These are to be the measure of our love toward others.

Yet we must not fall into the trap of thinking that our whole duty consists of loving others. We must remember that the first and greatest commandment is to love God with all our heart, soul, and mind. Through rightly loving God we are moved and enabled to love others rightly.

Christ, through his victorious resurrection, gave us the power to love as he loves. He left his spirit as his agent of that power in us.

> We know that we live in him and he in us, because he has given us of his Spirit. . . . Love is made complete among us so that we will have

confidence on the day of judgment, because in this world we are like him
(1 John 4:13-17).

Having received Christ's love, by the power of his Spirit who lives in
us, we are moved and enabled to be the hands and feet of God's love
on earth. What difference can this make in our world? Can Christ's
love be expressed toward individuals *and* societies and governments?

A Godlike love, the kind of love set forth in Scripture, establishes
the value of every person. Humans were created in God's image (Genesis 1:26-27), and each life is of great significance to God. A human
life is of such great significance that after Cain murdered his brother
Abel, God immediately asked Cain, "Where is your brother Abel? . . .
What have you done? Listen! Your brother's blood cries out to me from
the ground" (Genesis 4:9-10).

It was this value that prompted Job to query:

> "If I have denied justice to my manservants and maidservants
>   when they had a grievance against me,
> what will I do when God confronts me?
> What will I answer when called to account?
> Did not he who made me in the womb make them?
> Did not the same One form us both within our mothers?"
>
> —Job 31:13-15

Job expressed here that God, who made each one of us, treasures each
one of us. Though some may have more wealth and power in earthly
terms, everyone is of equal value to God. Job, who was a wealthy and
powerful man, realized that his wealth and power did not give him
liberty to violate the rights of others on earth. The Creator watches over
all people, values them, and holds accountable any who would transgress
against another.

Jesus took on human flesh, died on the cross, and rose again for the
sake of all persons. His actions give us our most powerful basis for
recognizing the value of persons, while also providing us with a match-
less model and the motivation for loving others.

> Your attitude should be the same as that of Christ Jesus:
> Who, being in very nature God,
>   did not consider equality with God something to be grasped,
> but made himself nothing,
>   taking the very nature of a servant,
>   being made in human likeness.
> And being found in appearance as a man,
>   he humbled himself
>   and became obedient to death—even death on a cross!
>
> —Philippians 2:5-8

God demands of us, then, that we show love to others as God has shown love to us. This recognition that God places value on each person and that God calls us, likewise, to value each person has brought humans to conceive of what we call basic human rights.

Basic human rights uphold the equality of all persons, the respect due to all persons, and the recognition that we all have common needs which should be met. Rights are not something that we demand from God. Rather, God demands from us that we recognize and protect the rights of other persons, in our personal interactions and in our corporate interactions as a church, as businesses, as organizations, and as a nation.

The demands of love upon us must be spelled out so that they are clear, firm, and permanent. We are fallen people, inclined to stretch or distort the demands of love to serve our own desires. For this reason, Jesus intensively taught his followers what the kingdom was like, what it stood for, and what it demanded of them. And for this reason, also, human governments find it necessary to codify what are acceptable and unacceptable actions.

We are motivated by love to uphold the basic human rights of others. Rights, in turn, form the fabric of justice. Paul Ramsey, in *Basic Christian Ethics,* defines love as "regarding the good of any other individual as more than your own when he and you alone are involved" and justice as "what Christian love does when it is confronted by two or more neighbors."[1] Because love affirms each person as being as valuable as each other person, love can proffer no reason for preferring the cause of one person over that of another. Yet sometimes a choice must be made between the conflicting demands on us of two or more different individuals. Justice aids love in such considerations by discerning among the conflicting claims.

For example, if you and your spouse were confronted by an attacker, love would see both your spouse and the attacker as being of equal value and as both deserving to live. However, justice would discern that your spouse has a higher claim on you and has the right to be protected from the attacker.

On a larger level, loving actions may be taking place within an evil society—as when, in a slave society, slave owners treat their slaves with kindness and generosity. But if the order of society is left unchanged, love is thwarted because the slave owners are being accorded human rights whereas the slaves are not. The standards of justice point out what the appropriate response of love would be in such a case: the restoring of equality to those who have been enslaved.

Love, then, is the basis of justice. Order is required for love to be carried out in human society. The rights accorded by love, the duty of upholding these rights, and the ordering of conflicting claims must be spelled out clearly and held to firmly. Justice carries out this task of providing the order that love requires.

Nevertheless, love goes beyond justice. Love is ultimately a higher good than justice because it gives justice its core, moral meaning. Justice is vital to carrying out the duties of love in society. Yet love provides the reason for the practice of justice. The work of love is never done. Love always goes the extra mile, beyond the requirements of justice, beyond the minimum required of us. It forgives the enemy; it turns the other cheek; it gives up its life for the sake of others.

Love restores weak persons and weak groups so that they can participate fully in mutual relationships. Jesus illustrated this working of love when he told the story of the good Samaritan.

. . . "A man was going down from Jerusalem to Jericho, when he fell into the hands of robbers. They stripped him of his clothes, beat him and went away, leaving him half dead. A priest happened to be going down the same road, and when he saw the man, he passed by on the other side. So too, a Levite, when he came to the place and saw him, passed by on the other side. But a Samaritan, as he traveled, came where the man was; and when he saw him, he took pity on him. He went to him and bandaged his wounds, pouring on oil and wine. Then he put the man on his own donkey, took him to an inn and took care of him. The next day he took out two silver coins and gave them to the innkeeper. 'Look after him,' he said, 'and when I return, I will reimburse you for any extra expense you may have'" (Luke 10:30-35).

The good Samaritan loved with his hands and his feet. Because he valued the life of the beaten person and respected his right to live, the Samaritan bound his wounds and took him to a secure place, where the wounds could heal. The story stops there, but love does not. A restoring, Christlike love not only binds people's wounds but turns to try to stop the source of attack. We are loving in a responsible way when we identify the causes of people's suffering and work to curtail them, when we in Christ's power confront social evil at its root in order to bring an end to it.

In summary, Jesus pointed out that God's will for us calls us to love God and to love one another. Christ gave us our greatest example of fulfilling these responsibilities. He showed God's love in word and deed, going so far as to lay down his life for us. As members of Christ's body we are to continue his ministry on earth, loving with our hands and feet. This love that we express respects and upholds the value of every person, and it works for their well-being. It brings us to recognize and uphold what we call basic human rights. These rights form the fabric of justice, that is, the demands of love in the social order, spelled out in clear and permanent form.

Therefore, upholding and executing justice is an expression of God's love and will. God's love not only ensures people of the minimum basic rights, but upbuilds people to a point of wholeness. It brings us not only to focus on immediate needs—"wounds"—but also to ensure a healthy and safe environment for all.

ENGAGE

Binding Wounds and Stopping Attacks

Turn back to page 15 and reread the part of "ENGAGE" entitled "What Can Be Done?"

1. Which of these types of action would you characterize as the binding of wounds? That is, which address mainly the suffering of individuals?

2. Which of these types of action would you characterize as turning to stop the attack? That is, which address the causes of social ills and suffering?

3. Could any of these types of action be a mixture of binding wounds and stopping attacks? Which ones, and in what way?

Many people prefer to involve themselves in the first two types of action, which mainly address the suffering of persons. While this suffering must be addressed, a deep and Christlike love cannot stop there. It must go on to address the causes of suffering. Often this requires voluntary group action and structural/institutional action, both focused to stop the evil where it makes its inroads.

Many projects can be conceived which include several types of action.

A good beginning for a church in social action would be for the church to adopt an elderly housing project in the town or a block of a low income housing project. The church then tries to get to know the residents as well as it can: visiting them, assuaging loneliness, and finding out what the people perceive as their needs. The church people then try to meet as many needs as they can by themselves or by involving the appropriate agency. Individuals or families can be paired up. There can be spiritual counselling, Bible studies, and provision of transportation to church. Immediate needs for transportation, material needs, and needs for referral to technical help are discerned and met. Co-ops can be formed. Aid is given to the residents in expressing and organizing their concerns about the structure and operation of their project and the general housing policy in the community . . . provision for varying degrees of involvement may prevent fragmentation and conflict because it allows people to become involved according to their level of social consciousness and their time and particular interest and gift.[2]

This example illustrates one way the members of a church might be moved to share with others the love that Christ has shared with them. It also illustrates how a ministry of Christian caring might begin with binding people's wounds, and then, prompted by a full and responsible love, turn to assess and address the structural causes of the suffering.

The Upholding of Rights

Take a recent copy of a newspaper or news magazine and look through it with the following questions in mind:

1. Which reports deal with people who are not being accorded basic human rights?

   (This could range from a report of a murder to a report of people being deprived of food, shelter, or jobs to a report about an oppressive government, etc. Be critical as you read, and cut out one or two articles to share with the group.)

2. Can you think of other situations, which were not covered in the paper, in which people are not being accorded basic human rights?

   (You might try to think about why these have not received media attention.)

3. Why are the rights of these individuals or groups not being upheld. What obstacles do you see?

4. What must be changed in order to achieve justice in these situations?

5. How might love go beyond the minimum demands of justice, to upbuild and fully restore the oppressed people?

My Role in Upholding Rights

Look again at the situations you discovered, in the news and on your own, in which people were being denied their basic human rights.

1. *How* might the above changes be made so that justice might be achieved? What type of action would it take?

2. Is it in your power to undertake or support this type of action? Why or why not? What, specifically, could you do?

3. What about prayer? Do you regularly pray for oppressed peoples and for ways in which you might work for their relief?

Make a commitment now, on paper, to take what actions you feel you can on behalf of some specific person(s) or group(s). It might take the following form:

● I will pray daily for . . . (list here those in need for whom you have a burden).

● Other actions I will take this week (appropriate to the needs of the above people):

1. send money to a relief organization;
2. contact my congressperson on their behalf;
3. attend a city council meeting as a supporter of their rights;
4. (you name it) . . . .

Report your faithfulness in keeping these commitments to your group during the next session. In the meantime, remember to support one another in prayer and in other ways in this undertaking.

4

The Creative Work
of Justice

"I hate, I despise your religious feasts;
I cannot stand your assemblies.
Even though you bring me burnt offerings and grain offerings,
I will not accept them.
Though you bring choice fellowship offerings,
I will have no regard for them.
Away with the noise of your songs!
I will not listen to the music of your harps."
—Amos 5:21-23

"The multitude of your sacrifices—
what are they to me?" says the LORD.
"I have more than enough of burnt offerings,
of rams and the fat of fattened animals;
I have no pleasure
in the blood of bulls and goats. . . .
When you spread out your hands in prayer,
I will hide my eyes from you;
even if you offer many prayers,
I will not listen."
—Isaiah 1:11, 15

Why would God, through the prophets, be saying these things? God addressed these words to the people of Israel, the very people bidden to come to God with sacrifices and burnt offerings, to come before God with song, and to pray unto God. These acts of devotion and praise were meant to be pleasing to God. Then God rejected these acts of religious devotion on the part of God's called-out people.

Pious acts are not enough; they only fulfill part of the divine covenant made with God's people. Unless religious worship is backed with true obedience, it is putrid in God's sight. Let's put these passages of Scripture in context and see what God demands.

> ". . . wash and make yourselves clean.
> Take your evil deeds
>   out of my sight!
> Stop doing wrong,
>   learn to do right!
> Seek justice,
>   encourage the oppressed.
> Defend the cause of the fatherless,
>   plead the case of the widow."
> —Isaiah 1:16-17
> "But let justice roll on like a river,
>   righteousness like a never-failing stream!"
> —Amos 5:24

The people of Israel had fallen away from a pure and true obedience to their God. They neglected the righteousness demanded of them. They cared little for doing good but were bent only upon serving their own interests. They ignored the demands of justice to protect the downtrodden, and they themselves became oppressors. Yet they still thought that they could maintain divine favor by meeting God in the temple. They thought they could appease and even please God with their empty acts of religious ritual.

We see the same thing occurring in the period of the New Testament, bringing Jesus to pronounce woes upon the Pharisees.

> "Woe to you, teachers of the law and Pharisees, you hypocrites! You give a tenth of your spices—mint, dill and cummin. But you have neglected the more important matters of the law—justice, mercy and faithfulness. You should have practiced the latter, without neglecting the former" (Matthew 23:23).

We cannot please God without obeying God's commands, without living according to the ethics of God's kingdom. If we neglect the more important matters of God's will, then our acts of religious worship will be empty as well. James wrote to the New Testament Christians that "Religion that God our Father accepts as pure and faultless is this: to look after orphans and widows in their distress and to keep oneself from being polluted by the world" (James 1:27). Here we see righteousness and justice again yoked together as the means of truly pleasing God.

While recognizing the centrality and vital importance of personal holiness, it is the purpose of this chapter to look at social justice as a mandate and as a means of pleasing God. Jesus listed justice as one of the "more important matters of the law," yet it is often neglected both as a focus of preaching and as a focus of Christian practice. What makes it such a vital element in truly obeying and pleasing God?

We see that justice is an attribute and an activity of God. This comes out many times in the Old Testament, which provided the foundation for our knowing and obeying God. Just a few sample passages follow.

> The King is mighty, he loves justice—
> you have established equity;
> in Jacob you have done
>   what is just and right.
> Exalt the LORD our God
>   and worship at his footstool;
> he is holy.
>   —Psalm 99:4-5

> The LORD works righteousness
>   and justice for all the oppressed.
> He made known his ways to Moses,
>   his deeds to the people of Israel.
>   —Psalm 103:6-7

> Blessed is he whose help is the God of Jacob,
>   whose hope is in the LORD his God,
> the Maker of heaven and earth,
>   the sea, and everything in them—
> the LORD, who remains faithful forever.
> He upholds the cause of the oppressed
>   and gives food to the hungry.
> The LORD sets prisoners free,
>   the LORD gives sight to the blind,
> the LORD lifts up those who are bowed down,
>   the LORD loves the righteous.
> The LORD watches over the alien
>   and sustains the fatherless and the widow,
> but he frustrates the ways of the wicked.
>   —Psalm 146:5-9

From these passages we learn not only about God's character and workings in the world. We also learn about the nature of the justice God exemplifies and executes and which, correspondingly, God expects from us.

There is one God. Since justice has its basis in God's character, there is therefore one justice for all people for all time. The justice we read about and are commanded to do in the Old Testament is confirmed and carried on in the New Testament. Its validity remains today as a standard and measure for us to follow.

It seems that most often, when the concept of God's justice finds its way into sermons, writings, and conversations, it is cast mainly as God's standard of judgment and punishment. While there is this aspect to God's justice, the picture presented in the Bible is also a positive, upbuilding one. God's justice flows from God's grace and is motivated by God's love. It acts to create and to preserve community, particularly by standing up for and aiding those who do not have power or resources of their own. Note the phrases in the preceding passages: "you have established equity"; "The LORD works righteousness and justice for all the oppressed"; "He upholds the cause of the oppressed and gives food to the hungry," etc.

Often, when the idea of judgment and punishment enter the biblical picture, as written in the prophets, God is judging and punishing the oppressors on behalf of the innocent and oppressed.

> You trample on the poor
> and force him to give you grain.
> Therefore, though you have built stone mansions,
> you will not live in them;
> though you have planted lush vineyards,
> you will not drink their wine.
> For I know how many are your offenses
> and how great your sins.
>
> You oppress the righteous and take bribes
> and you deprive the poor of justice in the courts.
> —Amos 5:11-12

Israel had defaulted on every aspect of its covenant with God. The people had ceased to love and worship the one true God who had brought them out of bondage; they had turned away from God's law; they had forsaken righteousness; they had neglected justice. Because of Israel's hardhearted lack of penitence, God brought judgment upon the people. Part of this judgment involved punishment for social injustice, as we read above. God's justice was not to be mocked.

Inherent in God's justice is a norm of equality. Things are the way they should be when everyone is able to participate fully and equally in the life of the society. When some are poor, without money or the means of making a living, something has gone wrong.* One of the basic rights accorded by love and protected by justice is the right to have one's essential needs met. If some are needy while others live in relative luxury, the latter are guilty of not upholding God's distributive justice.

There is a selfish human tendency to violate the norm of equality by accumulating wealth, even in the face of dire need, and to use that wealth to oppressive ends. We see this today, for example, when rich

---

*Rather than blaming the victims for their poverty, the Bible generally cites the cause of poverty as the oppression of the weak by those wielding power and wealth wrongly.

investors buy stocks in large corporations which exploit the natural resources and the laborers of poor, Third World countries. This exploitation leaves the poor in those countries even poorer, while the investors enjoy record profits and luxury living. We see this closer to home, as well, when money is invested in large banks that make loans to businesses at reasonable interest rates but refuse to make loans to needy people in poor neighborhoods. We see it also in the frivolous consumption by some of the earth's population—eating excessively protein-rich diets, buying processed foods in throwaway containers, and lavishing the same opulence on their pets—while much of the world's population goes hungry.

It is because of this hardhearted human tendency to disdain distributive justice that God's justice functions primarily on behalf of the disadvantaged. God calls humans to preserve and protect the rights of all. But if we forsake the needy, they will not remain forsaken. God will execute justice for them by cutting down the wealthy and bringing about redress. We see this bias toward the disadvantaged in the Beatitudes of Jesus.

> "Blessed are you who are poor,
>   for yours is the kingdom of God.
> Blessed are you who hunger now,
>   for you will be satisfied. . . .
> But woe to you who are rich,
>   for you have already received your comfort.
> Woe to you who are well fed now,
>   for you will go hungry."
> —Luke 6:20-25

This execution of justice for the needy involves a redistribution of resources. Here we see the creating, upbuilding hand of justice. The poor are to be provided with not only their immediate needs of food, shelter, and clothing; they are also to be equipped with a means of livelihood, so that they can participate equally in society. This redistribution occurs at the expense of the wealthy who profited from the distress of the needy, for their wealth was as out of line as was the poverty of the disadvantaged. As Mary, Jesus' mother, exclaimed, "He has filled the hungry with good things but has sent the rich away empty" (Luke 1:53).

How do we fit into this picture? What is our relationship to God's active, upbuilding justice? The answer is vital. God executes this creative, distributive justice through the obedience of God's people. When we follow God's example and commands and when we live according to the ethics of God's kingdom, we will be executing justice. We will be sensitive to the needy, loyal to the oppressed.

Just as we are able to act with Godlike grace toward others because of God's grace pouring into and through us, just as we are able to love others because of God's tremendous love, which motivates and enables us, so we are moved and enabled to execute God's justice. Grace, love, and justice all belong to the same family. They all extend from God as good gifts, which are given to transform and upbuild us and to be shared for the well-being, nurturance, and upbuilding of others, to the glory of God. We are to extend God's grace, love, and justice to others as God has extended them to us. We learn to do this by following God's example and heeding the guidance of God's commandments.

As we saw in previous chapters, God not only indicates how we should act toward others and motivates such action with gracious actions toward us, but God also gives us the ability to carry out God's will. This is true with justice just as it is with God's grace and love. We are able to give to the needy and stand up for the oppressed because God gives us the ability to do so. We are to be wise stewards of God's gifts. God's justice calls for distribution from each according to his or her ability, to each according to his or her *need*, not according to the worth, heredity, ability, or nobility of the recipient. This ultimately brings glory to God because the justice which we execute appears as grace to others since it was provided by a gracious God.

Not only are we called to do justice in our personal relations, but we are also called to take an active responsibility to see that justice is done in the wider community.

> So justice is driven back,
>   and righteousness stands at a distance;
> truth has stumbled in the streets,
>   honesty cannot enter.
> Truth is nowhere to be found,
>   and whoever shuns evil becomes a prey.
>
> The LORD looked and was displeased
>   that there was no justice.
> He saw that there was no one,
>   and he was appalled that there was no one to intercede. . . .
>   —Isaiah 59:14-16a

Situations of public injustice displease the Lord. Because of God's own character and activity, the people of God are called to imitate and obey God, intervening in unjust situations. It is appalling to God when we forsake that responsibility.

The Creative Work of Justice   47

Rather, we are to be active in seeking to correct the evil of oppression and to execute justice, for this is what our God desires and demands of us.

> "Is not this the kind of fasting I have chosen:
> to loose the chains of injustice
>   and untie the cords of the yoke,
> to set the oppressed free
>   and break every yoke?
> Is it not to share your food with the hungry
>   and to provide the poor wanderer with shelter—
> when you see the naked, to clothe him,
>   and not to turn away from your own flesh and blood?
>   and your healing will quickly appear;
> then your righteousness will go before you,
>   and the glory of the LORD will be your rear guard.
> Then you will call, and the LORD will answer;
>   you will cry for help, and he will say: Here am I."
>   —Isaiah 58:6-9a

We read something very similar in Matthew 25:31-56, where Jesus foretells the pronouncing of judgment according to how people treated the poor and needy of the earth.

> "Then the King will say to those on his right, 'Come, you who are blessed by my Father; take your inheritance, the kingdom prepared for you since the creation of the world. For I was hungry and you gave me something to eat, I was thirsty and you gave me something to drink, I was a stranger and you invited me in, I needed clothes and you clothed me, I was sick and you looked after me, I was in prison and you came to visit me. . . . I tell you the truth, whatever you did for one of the least of these brothers of mine, you did for me'" (Matthew 25:34-39).

We see here that God identifies with the poor and oppressed of the world, so much so that actions done or not done toward them are counted as actions done or not done toward God.

> " . . . But let him who boasts boast about this:
>   that he understands and knows me,
> that I am the Lord, who exercises kindness,
>   justice and righteousness on earth,
>   for in these I delight," declares the LORD.
>   —Jeremiah 9:24

We are to base our actions on what we know of God's own attributes, activity, and commands, siding with the poor and the powerless in the social struggles of our times.

To a certain degree we can carry out this responsibility through acts of private charity and through acts of personal ministry. When the number of sufferers becomes too large, however, private charity can't keep up with the ills of society. Love then requires that we use structural measures to achieve social justice. This involves the use of power in the cause of justice.*

The institutions of a society exert much influence in determining who receives the benefits and who bears the burdens of that society's life. Therefore we should bring our power to bear upon these institutions to ensure that their decisions favor the needy and disadvantaged and not the rich and powerful.**

Education provides a good example of this. Should the children of the rich be entitled to a better education than the children of unskilled laborers or welfare mothers? Should whites receive a better education than blacks, Hispanics, and other minorities? Should persons with special needs receive special treatment? Our social institutions make decisions such as these through the allotment of funds and the making and enforcement of policies. Since these institutions are supposed to be accountable to the public which supports them, organized groups of citizens can unite to make an impact upon policy and budgeting decisions. This applies to areas other than education as well.

When we are motivated by God's justice, we will realize a change in our eyes and in our hearts as we contemplate the world.

- We can then identify with the welfare mother whose real income decreases because the legislature avoids raising taxes by eliminating cost-of-living increases for welfare recipients.
- We shall appreciate the viewpoint of the black worker who fights prejudice to get a job only to lose it because the economics of treating inflation through increased unemployment often result in the last hired being the first fired.
- We shall feel the discouragement of the laborer who works full time yet remains in poverty.
- We shall share the frustration of the laborer who has seen the government he worked to elect overturned in a coup by elitest forces who had received support from the American government.
- We can feel the despair of a father in another land who gazes on the

---

*Power means the ability to accomplish something, even when opposed. Our power consists of our financial resources; our political influence as citizens of a democracy; our skills, abilities, and connections as members of a certain social class; our prestige; etc. Power can be increased by several means, including banding together with other people to pool resources, and gain numerical strength.

**In matters of criminal justice and court proceedings, however, all are to be treated equally.

marks of torture on the body of his son who died in prison and wonders why American dollars went to finance a dictatorship infamous for its violation of human rights.

• Our perspective will include the woman whose husband is dying of liver cancer probably caused by vinyl chloride, which has been produced in his country by his American employer after its production had been "too strictly regulated" in the United States. [1]

May we never lose this sensitivity. May we never lose a passion for God's justice, which moves us to do what we can to rectify situations that cause such suffering. May we never lose faith in the one true God, who empowers us to carry out God's will.

ENGAGE

Life-Style Analysis

It is a commonly known fact that Americans enjoy a standard of living much higher than that of the majority of the world community. We consume far more than our share of the world's rapidly depleting resources. Although we compose 6 percent of the world's population, we consume 30 percent of the world's resources. Not only is this imprudent from an ecological standpoint, but it is also unjust from a moral standpoint. Much of our wealth is derived from exploiting poor Third World countries by taking out more wealth and resources than we originally invested there; from private exploitation of public domain here in the United States, such as when the rights to oil-rich public lands are sold to private companies for one dollar; and from thoughtless technological expansion.

Are individual citizens of the United States responsible for the oppression and suffering caused by U.S. business, military, and government practices around the world? This is a difficult question. Insofar as we enjoy the products and benefits of these practices, we share in the responsibility.

It doesn't do much good to feel guilty in the face of this responsibility. A very diffuse type of social evil lies behind these practices and the resulting oppression; therefore the responsibility is diffuse. The important thing for us to see is that we have both a passive, negative responsibility for this situation and an active, positive responsibility to make the situation better, to fight the oppression and relieve the suffering. This active responsibility is the essence of God's distributive justice.

Awareness is the first step of a positive response; realizing that others go hungry while our pantries are well stocked; realizing that items we consider basic—like meat and toilet paper—are luxuries for many of the world's citizens; and realizing that hunger, pain, grief, and worry affect others with as sharp an intensity as they do us. That they suffer these feelings more often than we do does *not* mean that they are dulled to them. Another important part of this first step of awareness involves realizing that since we enjoy such relative wealth and power, God's distributive justice calls us to share this wealth and power in a way that will enable the poor and oppressed to lead full, productive lives.

A second step of active responsibility is *prayer*. We began this step in the last chapter—finding out who were suffering oppression and praying for them. It is vital for us to continue this process, thanking God for answered prayer and adding new people to our prayer list as we become aware of them. It is also important to personalize these prayers, asking God to use us and to guide us in executing justice for these people. (Remember, God doesn't expect us to save the world single-handedly; God does, however, expect us to be open and obedient to the Word and to God's leading.)

In the next section, entitled "The Responsible Use of Power," we will look at how we can mobilize our power and resources in more structural ways to help poor and oppressed peoples. In this section however, let us continue to examine how we might be actively responsible in the use of resources on a more personal level.

The advertising media and businesses encourage us to consume, consume and consume some more. They want us to equate buying things with being happy. This runs counter, however, to active ecological and moral responsibility in a finite world where many are suffering.

In Genesis 1:28 God gave to Adam and Eve—and, through them, to the human race—the responsibility of caring for and shepherding the earth. Though we have been poor stewards, we continue to have this responsibility to care for the earth. We also have a continuing responsibility to execute justice for the poor and oppressed. We must cling to these God-given duties even in the face of our culture's calls to violate them.

But how can we do this and still get along as members of our society? Do we have to give up everything and become destitute ourselves in order to be actively responsible to the poor? No, God does not call us to poverty, but we do have to begin to analyze our own life-styles critically and make some changes that will work toward greater equity for all persons.

Many Christians, sensitive to inequity in the world and to God's call to execute justice, are choosing a life-style of "voluntary simplicity." This involves putting a moratorium on the buying of unnecessary "things"; choosing to eat a diet that, calorie for calorie, uses less of the world's resources to produce; repairing, reusing, and recycling things rather than throwing them away and replacing them; finding joy and pleasure in developing gifts, using talents, and helping others rather than in spending money to bring pleasure to ourselves.

A life-style of voluntary simplicity can be enjoyed by institutions as well as individuals. Church buildings and equipment can be shared, for instance, among two or more congregations. The beauty of this life-style is that it cuts down on waste, replication, and needless buying; it makes us more responsible stewards of resources; and it aids the cause of justice by freeing resources which can be used to aid and empower those who have no resources. It puts us in touch with the *real* values of life, and makes us active partners with our Creator in spreading God's gracious provision to others.

Think about your life-style. What changes will you make to begin enjoying a life-style of voluntary simplicity, a responsible life-style that is of benefit to others? Any of the following publications can help you get started. They are rich with ideas for a full but simple life.

The Alternate Catalogue, second edition, (Ellenwood, Ga.: Alternatives, 1974)

Alternative Celebrations Catalogue, fourth edition (Ellenwood, Ga.: Alternatives, 1978)

These catalogues can be ordered from:

Resource Center and Bookstore
1124 Main St., P.O. Box 1707
Forest Park, GA 30050   phone: 404-361-5823

More-with-Less Cookbook, by Doris Janzen Longacre, (Scottdale, Pa.: Herald Press, 1976)

Living More with Less, by Doris Janzen Longacre, (Scottdale, Pa.: Herald Press, 1980)

These books can be ordered from:

Herald Press, Scottdale, PA 15683 or Kitchener, Ontario N2G 4M5.

How to Become a Poor Church and Save Faith, available from:
United Presbyterian Program Agency
Office of Social Education, Room 1101
475 Riverside Drive
New York, NY 10027

The Responsible Use of Power

Our resources, our political position, our social class status and our vocational prestige add up to power, our ability to bring about change, even in the face of opposition. As we saw above, at times it is necessary to bring about structural change in order for justice to be executed for the poor and oppressed. It is through the use of power that structural change is brought about.

Examples of using one's power to bring about change would be joining a lobbying group, such as Bread for the World, which researches and talks to policy makers about matters of world hunger; giving the extra resources that result from living a life-style of voluntary simplicity to a relief organization such as Church World Service or World Vision; writing letters to your congressional representatives and to the President of the United States concerning issues of justice; joining a community organization that is working to correct oppression in a specific area(s); campaigning actively for political candidates whose platforms and records show a concern for and a commitment to executing justice; joining a group, such as Amnesty International, that conducts letter-writing campaigns in the cause of seeking the rights of innocent political prisoners around the world; joining or starting a church social action committee to research and address local justice issues and the needs of those in the community. The list could go on and on; the opportunities are endless.

The point is not that every person should be doing all of these things. The point is to link your ability, your power, and your resources with others who are committed to working to correct oppression and to execute justice in a structural manner, lending clout to the side of justice on whatever issue you feel led to address. The point is to be actively responsible on behalf of those who have little or no power of their own.

The addresses for the groups mentioned above are as follows:

● Bread for the World—6411 Chillum Place, NW, Washington, DC 20012

● Church World Service—500 Main St., Box 188, New Windsor, MD 21776

● World Vision—919 West Huntington Dr., Monrovia, CA 91016

● Amnesty International/USA—2112 Broadway, New York, NY 10023
—3618 Sacramento St., San Francisco, CA 94118

Acting Responsibly

Now that you have begun to consider leading a more responsible life-style and using your power in responsible ways, it is time to commit yourself to taking concrete steps in that direction. Your commitment might take the following form:

I will take the following steps, beginning this week, toward a life-style of voluntary simplicity; possible steps include:

- eating more meatless meals;
- refusing to buy nonessential items, however appealingly they might be advertised;
- repairing and reusing items rather than throwing them out;
- recycling newspapers, cans, and bottles;
- learning to make certain essential items or foods rather than buying them ready-made.

I will devote freed resources to the following ends:

- freed time I will spend doing volunteer work for _____ (a specific organization);
- freed money I will give to _____(individuals or organizations);
- freed "things" I will donate to _____.

I will link my power with the following organizations:

in order to work for justice and correct oppression in the following ways:

Be ready to report back to your group during the next session. And, again, remember to support one another in this endeavor.

5

In the Service
of the King

He told them another parable: "The kingdom of heaven is like a mustard seed, which a man took and planted in his field. Though it is the smallest of all your seeds, yet when it grows, it is the largest of garden plants and becomes a tree, so that the birds of the air come and perch in its branches" (Matthew 13:31).

My husband and I live in Boston, half a block from what one *Boston Globe* columnist has said "could easily qualify as the meanest, most evil corner in town." "There," to quote his words, "at all turns of the clock, anything at all is for sale as long as it is not legal. Drugs, hard or soft; guns, loaded or unloaded; men, women, children, young or old; all can be bought. Any appetite can be satisfied. Any addiction fed."[1]

In our third-story apartment we have a small study with a window that looks out toward "the meanest corner." I often sit by that window to read, study, pray, or just watch the passersby. What a story many of their faces tell! Fear, pain, boredom, rebellion, emptiness, despair. I can easily grow discouraged, looking out my window. Satan's evil forces seem to be having a heyday, while I see little evidence of God's kingdom.

My "windows on the world"—newspapers, television, magazines— often bring the same discouragement. So much bad news, so much suffering, so little cause for rejoicing.

It is in the face of such discouragement at the seeming success of evil that we are called to live by faith. Just like a mustard seed planted in the ground, small and unseen, the kingdom of God is present in our midst in its power and potential. As surely as the seed will sprout and grow to huge proportions, so will God's kingdom sprout forth in greatness and glory.

God's kingdom is present here in my neighborhood. It is present in the members of Christ's body, the churches—proclaiming the gospel, ministering to the suffering, confronting the powers of evil, and glorifying God. Their influence may seem small in contrast to the influence of evil, but they labor in the power of God's promise that Christ will ultimately reign supreme.

Just what exactly is God's kingdom? How can it be already here but not yet here? Where do we fit in? What is our role and what is our responsibility?

The kingdom of God is not so much a place as an act of God.

The Greek word *basileia*, which is used for *reign* or *kingdom*, means primarily the *act* of reigning rather than the *place* of reigning; thus in most cases it should be translated as *reign, rule, kingship,* or *sovereignty,* rather than its usual English rendering, *kingdom.*[2]

It is God's kingship over all creation and God's rule over history. God's reign represents the promise and the expectation that God will ultimately establish complete dominion over all creation—that anything and everything that oppose God will be conquered.

In the Old Testament period Israel knew God as guardian and leader, as the king over all creation. The people expected and experienced God's reign in historical events, yet they looked forward to a fuller manifestation of God's rule in history. God's reign, coming in its fullness, would be characterized by justice and would mean both salvation and judgment for the people of Israel. They knew that they would be judged for their sinfulness on the one hand; on the other hand they expected God to deliver them from their national enemies, to give them new heart and new spirit so they might return to a faithful worship of God, and to establish justice once again. According to many prophecies, God would bring this about through an agent, later referred to as the Messiah. This Messiah would lead his people in obedience, would die for their iniquities, and would establish social justice.

> "Here is my servant, whom I uphold,
>   my chosen one in whom I delight;
> I will put my Spirit on him
>   and he will bring justice to the nations."
>   —Isaiah 42:1

This expectation of a fuller manifestation of God's reign through the Messiah, God's agent, was alive at the time of Jesus' conception and birth. We also see it in Mary's reaction to the miracle of God wrought within her (Luke 1:46-56) and in Simeon who, upon viewing Jesus,

took him in his arms and praised God, saying:
"Sovereign Lord, as you have promised,
    you now dismiss your servant in peace.
For my eyes have seen your salvation,
    which you have prepared in the sight of all people,
a light for revelation to the Gentiles
    and for glory to your people Israel."
                                        —Luke 2:28-32

We see the expectation in the prophetess Anna, who also recognized Jesus as the awaited Messiah.

Coming up to them at that very moment, she gave thanks to God and spoke about the child to all who were looking forward to the redemption of Jerusalem (Luke 2:38).

Long awaited by Israel and seen from afar by its prophets, the reign of God entered history in the person and the mission of Jesus Christ. The reign was present in Jesus' very being, and it was central to his ministry of teaching, healing, and casting out demons.

Once, having been asked by the Pharisees when the kingdom of God would come, Jesus replied, "The kingdom of God does not come visibly, nor will people say, 'Here it is,' or 'There it is,' because the kingdom of God is among you" (Luke 17:20-21).

Jesus' life and ministry, then, gave assurance of the presence of the reign. However in his proclamation of the reign he brought not only assurance, but a sense of urgency.

After John was put in prison, Jesus went into Galilee, proclaiming the good news of God. "The time has come," he said. "The kingdom of God is near. Repent and believe the good news!" (Mark 1:14-15).

The reign has come near. It means salvation to those who respond and doom to those who do not repent and submit to Christ's lordship. The time for decision and action is *now*, because the coming day of judgment and salvation is not long off (Mark 13:24-27).

Those who do repent must be watchful and ready when their Lord returns, obediently carrying out the tasks assigned them.

"Be on guard! Be alert! You do not know when that time will come. It's like a man going away: He leaves his house in charge of his servants, each with his assigned task, and tells the one at the door to keep watch.

Therefore keep watch because you do not know when the owner of the house will come back—whether in the evening, or at midnight, or when the rooster crows, or at dawn. If he comes suddenly, do not let him find you sleeping. What I say to you, I say to everyone: 'Watch!'" (Mark 13:33-37).

The assurance that Christ will return in glory and might to establish his full dominion over creation should lead us to a renewed diligence in carrying out his will. We live in the period between the small beginnings of the reign and its triumphant, magnificent end. We are to act as faithful servants of God, continuing the work of the reign as it was begun in Christ.

In Luke 4 we read the statement Jesus made at the beginning of his ministry, showing himself to be the Messiah and setting forth what his mission would be.

Jesus' proclamation of the reign involved both word and deed: preaching the Good News, healing the sick and handicapped, casting out demons, and freeing the oppressed. That he literally fulfilled the words from Isaiah 61:1-2 found in Luke 4:18-19 gave proof that Jesus was the promised agent of God's reign (see Luke 7:20-23). It also revealed that the reign is not solely spiritual, but that it extends to God's material creation as well—to human bodies and to social structures.

> We know that the whole creation has been groaning as in the pains of childbirth right up to the present time. Not only so, but we ourselves, who have the firstfruits of the Spirit, groan inwardly as we wait eagerly for our adoption . . . the redemption of our bodies (Romans 8:22-23).

Jesus' miracles of healing were not performed only as attention-getting devices to authenticate his proclamation of the Good News; they were an integral part of that Good News. To the Hebrews, physical healing was part and parcel of Jesus' message, along with economic or political deliverance; they saw the body as a person's link with the world, and disease as only one force by which it was assailed. Therefore healing was an act of justice, restoring a person's ability to function in society. It was essential to the proclamation of the reign. We read that Jesus sent his disciples out "to preach the kingdom of God and to heal the sick" (Luke 9:2). Healing, then, was an expression of God's active reign, extending not only to broken bodies but to other material factors which made people suffer (see Luke 4:18-19).

Jesus' healing and his casting out of demons were closely related in his ministry of proclaiming the reign. In Matthew 12:22-23, we read of an incident in which a demon-possessed man was brought to Jesus. The man was both blind and mute, but Jesus healed him so that he could talk and see. The Pharisees, who were present at this event, accused Jesus of casting out demons by the power of Satan. Jesus denied this, pointing to the poor logic of their accusation. Then he said, "But if I drive out demons by the Spirit of God, then the kingdom of God has come upon you" (Matthew 12:28).

Jesus identified his power and his purpose in casting out demons with the rule of God. His mission of proclaiming the reign constantly brought him into conflict with the forces of evil. The demons themselves clearly recognized the threat which the presence of the reign posed to them.

> When Jesus stepped ashore, he was met by a demon-possessed man from the town. For a long time this man had not worn clothes or lived in a house, but had lived in the tombs. When he saw Jesus, he cried out and fell at his feet, shouting at the top of his voice, "What do you want with me, Jesus, Son of the Most High God? I beg you, don't torture me!" (Luke 8:27-28).

> Just then a man in their synagogue who was possessed by an evil spirit cried out, "What do you want with us, Jesus of Nazareth? Have you come to destroy us? I know who you are—the Holy One of God!" (Mark 1:23-24).

The demons recognized Christ as the rightful king over creation, come to destroy every power in opposition to the will of God. This spelled their doom, for his power was much greater than theirs.

Jesus shared his mission and his power over the demonic with his earliest followers:

> The seventy-two returned with joy and said, "Lord, even the demons submit to us in your name."
> He replied, "I saw Satan fall like lightning from heaven. I have given you authority to trample on snakes and scorpions, and to overcome all the power of the enemy; nothing will harm you. However, do not rejoice that the spirits submit to you but rejoice that your names are written in heaven" (Luke 10:17-20).

The power over the demonic had a purpose: the establishment of God's rule. The disciples were not to lose this sense of purpose in their exercise of God's power. Rather they were to cling to this purpose of establishing the reign, rejoicing in their citizenship under God's sovereign rule.

For a short while Jesus' crucifixion appeared to his followers to mean that he had been defeated by the evil forces. However his resurrection on the third day confirmed his victory once and for all (Hebrews 2:14-15, Romans 6:9).

Christ is king. He reigns, but at present he is only partially governing. The rebellion against God continues; the decisive battle against the powers of evil will not be won until after Christ returns. In the meantime it is God's purpose to continue the work that Christ began through his corporate body, the church. We are to exercise Christ's power in proclamation of his reign just as he did while he was on earth in human form.

Again Jesus said, "Peace be with you! As the Father has sent me, I am sending you." And with that he breathed on them and said, "Receive the Holy Spirit. If you forgive anyone his sins, they are forgiven; if you do not forgive them, they are not forgiven" (John 20:21-23).

We are to preach the Good News of salvation, to bring healing, to oppose the forces of evil, to establish justice, and to make disciples. These are not separate tasks, but several facets of the one task of proclaiming Christ's reign. As we set ourselves to this task, we must remember our purpose as Christ admonished his disciples, rejoicing in our citizenship under God's rule.

We must take care not to fall into extremes. On the one hand, there is the pitfall of neglecting to carry out the proclamation of the reign in the social sphere, thinking that society does not merit the effort because it is temporal. By the same reasoning, our bodies are temporal, they will ultimately die, and so it is not worthwhile to care for them. But this is absurd. We are to care for our bodies as parts of God's creation and as temples of the Holy Spirit; and just as we care for our bodies, so we should care for our social institutions as aspects of God's creation and as instruments for good or for evil in the lives of human beings. We would not think of neglecting to work toward personal holiness while we wait for Christ's return; neither can we dare to neglect working for holiness in our social structures. We are called to execute justice as a demand of Christ's rule; it is part of the creator's constitutional order for every creature. Christ calls his servants to be diligent in carrying out God's will until the time of his return.

At the same time we must avoid the pitfall of thinking that we will be able to build a perfect society in history. This simply cannot and will not be achieved by our efforts. *We* do not create the reign or build it up, *God* does. We are God's servants, instruments in this effort. We receive the reign as a gift, but with it comes the demand and the power to be channels of God's creation. The reign is not a social program. However, faithfulness to the reign's demand for justice makes social programs and social struggle necessary when we come into conflict with the forces of evil that are present in our social structures. The reign is both the standard toward which we work and the context within which we work.

In the seriousness of our task, we must not forget that the service of the reign is a service of joy.

"The kingdom of heaven is like treasure hidden in a field. When a man found it, he hid it again, and then in his joy went and sold all he had and bought that field" (Matthew 13:44).

The reign of Christ deserves and demands our all; let us give ourselves freely as true servants of the king.

ENGAGE

Continuing Christ's Work

If Christ had come to North America in the twentieth century, rather than to Palestine two thousand years ago, to proclaim his reign,

1. where would he see oppression and suffering and injustice?
2. how might he respond in order to bring healing and execute justice?
3. who would feel threatened by Jesus' presence and his ministry?
4. who would oppose Jesus and try to entrap him?

You might want to role-play this situation. Have one person act as Jesus and another person act as an interviewer, trying to get Jesus' perspective on the contemporary scene and/or on a specific event in recent news. You might want to rephrase the above questions to get at specific issues; for example: "Jesus, what do you see as the gravest problem(s) in North America (or your community) today?" "What do you intend to do about it?" etc.

Since we, the church, are Christ's body on earth today,' it is highly relevant for us to try to see things as Christ might. Consider the following questions.

1. Does Christ's church really see things as Christ might see them today?
2. If not, what impedes it? (If answer to question 1 is yes, go on to question 3)
3. Is the church responding to contemporary situations as Christ would respond?
4. If not, what impedes it? If yes, what results do we see?

The Struggle Demands Strategy

As Christ's body continuing his ministry on earth, we also find ourselves continuing Christ's struggle against the demonic. As we saw in chapter 1, the forces of evil take hold at various specific locations in society; thus they must be combatted with specific strategies.

In the second part of "Engage," chapter 1, you were asked to record your answers to specific questions about what evil and suffering God might see in your world and call you to respond to. Refer to page 15 now and reread these questions and your recorded answers. Would you make any additions or changes in light of what you have learned since then?

Now look at the section "What Can Be Done," also on page 15. Which type(s) of action would you choose to employ in your struggle with the demonic in each of the specific situations you have cited? Would you use a combination of any of these types of action? Explain your choice(s).

Review and Assessment

Report to the group your experience in beginning a life-style of voluntary simplicity—the changes you made, your reactions, and your dreams or plans for further changes.

Brainstorm together on how the group might cooperate to support the simpler life-styles of its members. (For example, you might decide to begin a food co-op or a skills exchange, in which people share their expertise in various areas such as carpentry, plumbing, sewing, etc.)

Report on your experiences so far in using your power to help oppressed peoples—the actions you have taken, any results you have had, your plans or dreams for further actions, your need for more information or more support in order to act more effectively. Could any or all of the group members team up in a certain area to pool power and resources?

6

Caring in Word and Deed

(Before beginning to read this chapter, turn to the first part of "Engage" on page 71, and complete the "Attitude Inventory.")

He threaded his way down the crowded street. A tall, striking man, he stood out among the throng. His long, sure strides carried him rapidly while his intense grey eyes kept pace, taking in everything about him. The heat of the July night had brought the residents of this East London slum out onto the streets: barefoot peddlers trying to earn their suppers; children foraging in piles of rotten fruit under produce market stalls; men and women flocking in and out of pubs, weaving around drunken children and fighting men; prostitutes; soldiers; sickly babies; toughened seamen.

William Booth took it all in. He was no stranger to poverty. At thirty-six years of age, married and the father of six, Booth lacked in almost everything but character and compassion. Yet as he walked this street, Booth was not thinking of his own poverty. The misery of these people compelled his attention. Here he saw not only a poverty of pocket but also a poverty of soul. As he walked, the different strands of the evangelist Booth's vision coalesced. "Darling," he burst out to his wife as he arrived home, "I've found my destiny."[1]

And what a destiny! It began with the Christian mission in East London's slums, a work which aimed to help and to convert the forgotten people whom the churches did not reach. Booth and his wife, Catherine, nurtured that seed of vision with their faith and obedience, dedicating their lives to meeting human need. Their eyes seemed to see people that the rest of their society either ignored or exploited. As the hands and feet of Jesus, they reached out and ministered to these people, meeting spiritual and physical needs alike.

God blessed the ministry of the Booths and increased their vision. Many felt called to join them in their evangelistic efforts and in their caring ministry to broken people. Eventually, they took for themselves the name "Salvation Army," a name which today encompasses a worldwide evangelistic and service organization.

From its earliest days the Salvation Army focused on evangelistic efforts among society's cast-offs. As a gifted evangelist, William Booth had a deep concern for souls. He wanted these forgotten people to hear the Good News of Christ and to experience personally Christ's liberation from sin and death. Yet Booth also had a practical concern, expressed in his famous quote, "You can't preach to a man on an empty stomach."[2] Thus Booth's concern for needy souls led directly and immediately to a concern for needy bodies.

"This is the way it grew," William Booth would correct those who saw it all as a planned campaign. "We saw the need. We saw the people starving, we saw people going about half-naked, people doing sweated labour; and we set about bringing a remedy for these things. We were obliged—there was a compulsion. How could you do anything else?"[3]

Much of the work of the Salvation Army, from its inception until today, has involved ministering to individuals with deep physical as well as spiritual needs—the destitute, the disabled, those addicted to drugs and alcohol, those caught in vice, those with mental problems. People unlovely and unreached by churches, yet precious to the Savior.

As Booth became ever more aware of the magnitude of need and the number of forgotten people, he developed creative solutions that involved institutional action at various levels. When Booth saw men sleeping out on the street on frigid winter nights, he set up shelters and kitchens where the destitute could count on getting lodging and nutritious, low-cost meals. He had the vision; God provided the means.[4]

Booth became aware of exploitation in Britain's match factories—women and children working sixteen-hour days, earning a pittance, and suffering exposure to yellow phosphorus, which eventually ate away their jaws and resulted in death. His concern moved him to set up well-lit, airy factories that employed people to make matches using harmless red phosphorus. Booth didn't stop there; intent on reforming the industry, he drew the attention of journalists and politicians to the situation. He didn't win immediate victory, but the Salvation Army proved itself to have staying power. The organization eventually saw its goal reached when the last match factory gave up using the destructive yellow phosphorus. Booth and his Army cared about the physical health and wholeness of the people with whom they wanted to share the Good News of Christ.[5]

Booth and his organization found that championing the cause of the powerless did not lead to public popularity. Fortunately, they were not out to win a popularity contest. They were out to save souls and to seek justice. One of their most risky and hotly disputed forays involved their efforts to break Britain's prostitution racket. Booth's daughter-in-law, Florence, administered a home for girls who were reclaimed from prostitution. She did all she could to heal their lives in Christ's love and power. Yet she could not rest knowing that each day more and more innocent young girls were being kidnapped and forced into lives of captive prostitution. Her concern spurred her husband, Bramwell Booth, to seek the aid of a powerful newsman and friend, William T. Stead. Through daring investigation, in which he was aided by Salvation Army personnel, Stead came out with a powerful news exposé which rocked the country. This exposé led to the passage of legislation that protected the powerless innocent, despite the opposition of powerful exploiters.[6]

William Booth and his Salvation Army knew that social conditions have a lot to do with physical and spiritual health or illness. He knew that there were environments in which "vice has an enormous advantage over virtue" and whose influence, summed up, was "atheism made easy."[7] Booth and his Army confronted sinful individuals and structures, but not on their own power. General Booth wrote, "The Scheme of Social Salvation is not worth discussion which is not as wide as the Scheme of Eternal Salvation set forth in the Gospel."[8]

Thanks to William and Catherine Booth and those who have had the courage to join them, the healing touch of the Salvation Army reaches around the world today. Every major city in the United States knows the blessing of its presence. The Salvation Army harbors the homeless, helps the addicted, befriends the friendless, and, by these means, gives powerful evidence of the reality and nature of the Christ whom its members communicate.

Evangelism. Witnessing. Sharing our faith. There are several labels, but they all refer to one process: telling the Good News of the death and resurrection of Jesus Christ, God's Son, in whose person and work the reign of God has broken into history. Few would question that every Christian has a responsibility to proclaim this Good News. We find that part of our very nature as new creatures is the desire to glorify the One who changed us and made us new. God's Spirit brings this about in us, transforming us until Jesus graces our words and our lives.

Some people feel that evangelism is the only responsibility that Christians have in the world. We must share our faith with unbelievers, telling them how they can know Jesus Christ as their Savior. We must back up our witness with a pure life. Then we have done all that God expects of us.

People who feel this way generally believe that the way to make society better and more just is to bring about more conversions. They believe that as more and more individuals come to a saving faith in Christ, society will automatically be upgraded.

We examined this perspective in the "Engage" section of chapter 1 when we pondered the question of why God didn't free the people of Israel from Egypt by having them witness to their captors. Evangelism is decidedly a central function of God's people on earth, but does it stand alone as God's plan for us?

A balanced reading of the whole of Scripture would have us answer no. Evangelism does not stand alone as God's plan for us. We dare not neglect it, for it is a responsibility of each one of us individually and of all of us corporately. Yet neither do we dare to neglect God's commands that we seek justice. They are equally biblical; they are equally compelling.

The view that evangelism alone fulfills our duty in the world and is the only path to justice rests on an unbiblical optimism. For one thing, it overestimates the number of conversions that will occur. Jesus did not suffer from such a delusion. His comment, " . . . when the Son of Man comes, will he find faith on the earth?" (Luke 18:8) bespeaks a realism about the prospects for Christian growth.

This view also overestimates the degree of Christlikeness which the new converts will attain. Jesus told the parable of the sower and the seed to forewarn his disciples about such optimism (Luke 8:4-15). The gospel brings varying responses, even among those in whom it takes root.

Some who see evangelism as the sole cure for our social problems tend to deny the importance of the physical self while emphasizing the spiritual self. The conditions that the physical self must endure don't matter as long as the spiritual self is healthy. The faith of people holding this view would not motivate them to seek a cure for cancer so much as it would motivate them to comfort the sufferer and pray for recovery. It would not motivate them to campaign for better working conditions so much as it would motivate them to make sure the worker is thinking clean thoughts and witnessing to co-workers. They bind wounds, but they let the attacks continue.

Yet we have seen that stopping the attacks is also part of our duty as citizens of God's reign. God's Word affirms the unity of each person. The distinction between physical and spiritual self comes from Greek thought, not biblical thought. The Bible acknowledges that the suffering of the body affects the whole person, and likewise the renewal of the spirit affects the whole person. Again we note Jesus' ministry of healing that touched body and soul alike. Jesus' victory over sin and death transforms the whole person, or else how could Paul say, " . . . we ourselves, who have the first fruits of the Spirit, groan inwardly as we wait for our adoption as sons, the redemption of our bodies'' (Romans 8:23, RSV)?

Others who hold that evangelism is the only solution to social problems don't necessarily see a division between the physical and spiritual self. They see the transformation of one's whole self having a ripple effect: as one is changed on the inside, that change is expressed in social relationships, and eventually society is changed.

There are two problems with this perspective. For one thing, it sees the influence flowing in only one direction, from the individual to society. This ignores the tremendous influence that our society has upon us as individuals and groups. Biblical accounts, sociological studies, and our own experiences show that people tend to conform to the expectations of the groups of which they are a part. Think of your own life—your life in your family, your church, your workplace, your community, your country. Think of how your behavior varies from group to group. Even when you have different values from the rest of the people in the group, so that you do not conform to their behavior, their norms as a group still exert influence upon you. They cause you to reexamine your values, so that you change them or defend them.

We see, then, that society exerts influence upon each one of us. (For what is society but the totality of the groups of which we are a part, a totality which becomes an entity unto itself and exerts further influence upon us?) The view that sees social problems being solved merely through the indirect influence of Christian individuals ignores this important dimension of social reality.

This view also ignores the structural reality of sin. We have seen that sin is not just an individual matter or a matter of personal relationships. It also takes root in our social structures. It is not enough, then, for an individual to live a pure life. That focus on individuals alone stems from Western culture, not from God's Word. Scripture calls Christians to live holy lives as part of a called-out community. God's law and covenant were given to a community, the people of Israel. Similarly, God's new covenant and God's Spirit were given to a new community, the church.

Just as we experience our faith individually and corporately, we must live it out in like manner, confronting sin individually and corporately. As the body of Christ, we must be the light that flushes evil from our social structures and the salt which preserves society from moral rot.

Evangelism cannot stand alone. But neither can social action. As the pendulum has swung in the history of Christianity, there have been those who have committed themselves to one aspect of the gospel. Those concentrating on social expression found themselves with spiritually bankrupt churches. Those adhering to an evangelism-only stance have largely withdrawn from the spiritually bankrupt institutions and practices of their society.

Our social action comes to naught without witness. It bears seedless fruit, for where Christ is left out, there is no life. Those involved in such action ultimately burn out.

Likewise, without social action, words of witness may fall short of their mark. When witness is backed up with social action, the Good News is more likely to get through because it is seen, heard, and felt.

Missionaries have long known the importance of integrating witness and social action. They use ministries of physical caring, such as medicine and agriculture, to create opportunities for telling the Good News and as evidence of Christ's love which supports their words.

Social action helps get believers out of "Christian ghettos" and into the world. The formulators of the Evangelism Explosion ministry have noted a phenomenon which they call "lift." They have observed that Christians tend to find themselves increasingly "lifted" out of contact with unbelievers.

> The longer you are a believer, the more opportunity you have for spiritual growth. The more you grow spiritually, the more involved you become in the life of the church. The more you are involved in the life of the church, the less opportunity you will have to be involved with non-Christians.[9]

As a corrective to this phenomenon of "lift," involvement in ministries of social caring helps Christians to have more contact with those who have not yet made a commitment to Christ Jesus; it opens up opportunities for evangelism that we might not otherwise have.

Moreover, social action helps to protect the fruit of witness. It helps to create and maintain a social atmosphere in which the potential for Christian growth and wholeness is maximized.

John Perkins was born poor and black in rural Mississippi in 1930. His mother died of pellagra, a disease caused by a nutritional deficiency, when he was seven months old, and his father left the family soon thereafter. John was left in the custody of sharecropping relatives who made extra money through bootlegging and gambling.

Until John reached sixteen, his life consisted mainly of hard work in the fields, with perhaps three months of school per year wedged in besides. When he was sixteen, a major turning point came in John's life. His brother was killed by a town sheriff without apparent cause. John's relatives decided to send John away to protect him from a similar fate; they scraped some funds together and put him on a train to California.

John made the most of the new opportunity. Before he was thirty he had proved himself in the work world. Despite his fifth grade education, he had a good job with room for advancement. He had married a girl from back home, and she was on the way to owning her own beauty shop. Together they had bought a home of their own—a first for John's family—and they had begun to have children.

At this period in his life, John came to know Jesus Christ as his personal savior. His wife, Vera Mae, recommitted her life as well. They immediately began volunteering time to teach Bible classes for children, to do home visitation, and to lead worship services, etc. They saw many people accept Christ as Savior and Lord through their ministry.

In the midst of this flurry of involvement, John began to sense the Lord calling him to return to Mississippi, to leave their home, jobs, friends, church, and the relative racial freedom of California. John wasn't sure what his ministry back in Mississippi would involve, but he had a burden for the black church and he had a burden for those who hadn't heard the Good News of liberation in Christ.

June, 1960, found John, Vera Mae, and their children living in Mississippi. They began their work by organizing vacation Bible schools. They received such a fantastic response that in the fall they set up Bible classes in local black schools and at a local black junior college. Eventually they themselves established a school, the Voice of Calvary Bible Institute.

The Perkinses and those who had joined with them in ministry found that their concern to evangelize led them naturally to acts and programs addressing social concerns. In John's own words,

Through our evangelism, the Lord had taken us into the very lives of people. Into their hearts and into their homes, bringing us face to face with their needs.

We saw that people could not read the Bibles and the tracts we gave them. We saw children who could not think because they had not had enough to eat. We saw conditions in people's homes that would keep them from ever getting well once they got sick.

These were some of the needs our people had. The needs they really felt. We saw them, too. And we moved to meet them.[10]

The Voice of Calvary Ministries (VOC), as their work came to be known, became active in helping blacks register to vote, so that they could better their lives through participating in the political process which had so long been closed to them. Some of the Perkinses' friends and supporters in black and white evangelical churches were not sure that voter registration should be part of a Christian ministry. As one friend queried, "The whole idea of you going back there was to get people saved. Don't you think you are getting away from that?"[11]

John thought long and hard on that and similar questions. He concluded that, no, he wasn't getting away from his original intent. Rather, he was carrying out the full implications of the gospel, which he had returned to Mississippi to proclaim.

As the Perkinses continued to evangelize, they also continued to confront the many needs of the rural poor of Mississippi. Through God's guidance they came up with many innovative plans for addressing those needs.

Near the end of 1967 John became active in organizing cooperatives, with a view to developing local resources and local income. They began with housing in Mendenhall, where they carried out their ministry. With local funds and matching Farmers' Home Administration funds, the co-op built ten duplex units. In the process the community gained not only better housing, but also leadership training, local pride, self-esteem, and a chance rarely given to the poor—a chance to take part in their own economic betterment.

An agricultural supplies co-op and a cooperative store soon followed the housing co-op, and in 1972-1973 VOC organized a cooperative health center.

In a forward-looking effort to multiply the effects of VOC's ministry, John Perkins set up the VOC Leadership Development Program in 1968. It provides young volunteers the opportunity to work in VOC's ministries. Through study, hands-on experience, and working side-by-side with VOC's leaders, they gain skill, strategical know-how, and discipline in living out the implications of God's reign.

Voice of Calvary has grown and evolved by the grace of God since

John and Vera Mae Perkins returned to Mississippi in 1960. It is now considered a model for community development. The three thrusts of VOC's strategy include: evangelism, social action, and visible community development. According to John Perkins,

> Evangelism creates the committed people, the concern for needs of people and the broad community base from which to launch social action. Social action, in turn, fleshes out the Lordship of Christ, reaching people's spiritual needs through their felt needs and developing an indigenous economic base for the work.[12]

In John Perkins's model we can see a cycle that begins with evangelism, the sharing of the Good News of Christ. This cycle leads the carriers of Good News immediately and automatically into social action. Social action forms the foundation for community development. As the process continues, people inquire about the motivation of the enthusiastic, loving people working so hard to help them. Thus the Good News comes full circle—through a ministry of caring, in Christ's name in word and deed.

ENGAGE

Attitude Inventory

Read through the following statements and check those that most nearly state your views.

_____ 1. I believe that if persons verbally share the gospel with others, they are fulfilling their duty as Christians.

_____ 2. I believe that it is not important for Christians to share the gospel verbally as long as they live out the gospel by trying to make life better for others.

_____ 3. I believe that persons cannot separate the strands of evangelism and deeds that help others, for they are interwoven to make up the Christian's duty.

_____ 4. I believe that Christians have no business seeking social change.

_____ 5. I believe that Christians should seek social change but that their attempts to do so must necessarily differ from those of the world.

_____ 6. I believe that the only way to bring about social change is through witnessing to individuals.

_____ 7. I believe that social change can only be brought about through structural action and legislation.

_____ 8. I believe that social change is best brought about through a combination of evangelism and structural action.

Once you have completed the inventory, turn back to page 63 and read through the narrative section of chapter 6.

Taking Stock of Your Attitudes

Now that you have read the chapter, look over the answers you gave to the attitude inventory. Has reading the chapter
a) caused you to change any of your viewpoints? Which ones? Why?
b) helped clarify your views?
c) reaffirmed the views you already held?
d) helped you back up your views with examples and arguments?

Your attitudes are important because they are a major part of what guides your behavior. Jesus said, "The things that come out of the mouth come from the heart . . ." (Matthew 15:18). What we say and what we don't say, what we do and what we don't do, evidence our values, thoughts, and feelings. It is important to be in touch with our attitudes, so that we can exercise greater control over our behavior.

While it is true that our attitudes guide our behavior, it is also true that our behavior can alter our attitudes. Our beliefs and feelings sometimes tag along behind our behavior until we change those attitudes to bring them into unity with our actions. For instance, when a Christian begrudgingly but consistently obeys a command of Jesus, his or her attitudes gradually change to become more Christlike, until the person obeys willingly and cheerfully.

What do your responses to the attitude inventory say about your behavior? Are you acting upon your beliefs? Do both your attitudes and your actions measure up to the commands of Christ?

Case Study

How would you respond to the following case study?

Robert Schuller is the pastor of the Garden Grove Community Church in Orange County, California. Begun in 1955 in a drive-in movie theater, the church is now housed in the famed Crystal Cathedral, located on twenty-three acres of ground. The congregation numbers in the thousands, while viewers of the *Hour of Power* television program, originating in the church, number in the millions.

Dr. Schuller voices the purpose of the church as, "Find a hurt and heal it.'' The hurts which are found are mainly individual hurts—divorce, alcoholism, sickness, the sense of futility, and lack of confidence in oneself. How are they healed? Through "possibility thinking." Dr. Schuller, in his books and sermons, tells over and over of people to whom God has given impossible dreams and made them come true. As a result, these persons have been very successful in helping others.

Great resources of material power . . . an emphasis on the possibilities of spiritual power . . . a voiced concern about healing the hurts of others. . . . What potential for addressing the concerns of social justice, in Christ's name! Let's see how Dr. Schuller responds to those concerns.

A visitor to Dr. Schuller's office on the fifteenth floor of the Tower of Hope, from which it is possible to see a large portion of Orange County, once criticized the famous pastor for being a "Johnny-one-note" preacher. After a moment of uncertainty about how to respond to the accusation, Dr. Schuller said:

"Of course, that's who I am. That's what the gospel calls for. One note of Good News. All things are possible with God."

"But I am interested in how you handle that note," said the visitor. "How do you translate that message in terms of social justice?"

"I am not sure what you mean," Dr. Schuller replied.

"Well, suppose you discover that the prison in Orange County is the most inhumane and corrupt of all penal institutions. How would you use the clout of this church to deal with that?"

"I would only try to convert the jailer," he said, adding that he refused to allow his church to become involved in controversial issues of the civil order.

The visitor persisted. "But suppose you looked again and discovered that the real 'jailer' is not a specific person, the warden of the prison, but is really the combined social and political forces of the whole state of California; that jails are what they are because people want them that way."

"I wouldn't know how to deal with that," said the pastor.[13]

Based on what you have read in this chapter:

1. What is the basis for the strategy Dr. Schuller said he would use for prison reform?

2. Do you feel it is a sufficient strategy? What is right or wrong with it?

3. How would you respond to the last challenge of the visitor, that perhaps the real 'jailer' is not one specific person?

4. How might the resources and concerns of a church such as this one be brought to address social justice issues, such as the one of prison reform suggested in the interview?

—What views would have to change?

—What new insights would be necessary?

—What organization would be needed?

5. Dr. Schuller raised an important issue when he said he refused to allow his church to become involved in controversial issues of the civil order. (Record your thoughts, because this is one of the issues we will deal with in chapter 7.)

—Do you feel prison reform is a controversial issue?*

—Do you feel that churches have the right to become involved in issues of the "civil order"?

To Know Me Is to Love Me

By now you have come to know one another better as a group through the time you have spent together and through your sharing in the various "Engage" activities. You have experienced agreement, disagreement, and perhaps even open conflict.**

Now it is time to get to know one another even better through a sharing of what makes each one of you "tick." Refer to "More on Motivation," on page 29, and also to the "Attitude Inventory" in this chapter. Each of you should share with the whole group

1. what you believe about the roles of evangelism and social action in your responsibility as a Christian;

2. which of the five descriptions on page 30 best describe you right now;

3. which of the five types of people on page 30 you would like to become.

The group as a whole should listen carefully and courteously to what each person has to say. No one should criticize or belittle any person because of what he or she shares. When you have shared, the group as a whole should discuss the following questions:

1. As a group, how can we support one another in a way that will help each one grow in motivation, in commitment, and in ability?

2. Do we as a group share a consensus of opinions, or do our opinions diverge so widely that we would be better off breaking up into

*Can we expect the reign of God and the earthly rule of the adversary to intersect without resulting in controversy?

**A good book for dealing with conflict and conflict resolution is *When You Don't Agree*, by James G. T. Fairfield (Scottdale, Pa.: Herald Press, 1977).

mutually supportive groups for the action components of our time together?

—What would be lost if this were done?

—What would be gained if this were done?

—Do the gains outweigh the losses?

3. Are the members of our group already involved in various types of socially caring ministry? If so, are we more inclined to function as a support group—in which we meet to support one another in our various ministries through prayer, worship, sharing of ideas and resources, and mutual accountability—than as an action group which would involve us in one more activity?

4. Given the motivation and commitment of our group or groups, what type or degree of action can we realistically expect to accomplish? (As you discuss this question, don't leave out the factor of God's transcendent and miraculous grace, which can change people and multiply their efforts. Remember the lessons of Gideon and of the boy with the loaves and fishes!)

For further reading on the subject of evangelism consider the following resources:

Hunter, George, *The Contagious Congregation: Frontiers in Evangelism and Church Growth.* Nashville: Abingdon Press, 1979.

Kennedy, James, and Parrish, Archie B., *Evangelism Explosion,* rev. ed. Wheaton, Ill.: Tyndale House Publishers, 1977.

Peace, Richard, *Witness.* Grand Rapids: The Zondervan Corporation, 1971.

Pippert, Rebecca M., *Out of the Salt Shaker: Evangelism as a Way of Life.* Downers Grove, Ill.: Inter-Varsity Press, 1979.

Watson, David, *I Believe in Evangelism.* Grand Rapids: Wm. B. Eerdmans Publishing Co., 1977.

7

God's People for God's Purposes

But you are a chosen people, a royal priesthood, a holy nation, a people belonging to God, that you may declare the praises of him who called you out of darkness into his wonderful light. Once you were not a people, but now you are the people of God; once you had not received mercy, but now you have received mercy (1 Peter 2:9-10).

The New Testament presents over a score of images illustrating the nature and mission of God's called-out people, the church. The predominant image, coming from the writings of Paul, portrays the church as the body of Christ. Gifted and empowered by the Holy Spirit, the church bears Christ's image and represents him on earth. Our presence, our proclamation, our unity amidst diversity, our multiplicity of abilities and functions all reflect Christ and continue, by his power, the mission which he initiated.

In Jesus Christ, the reign of God broke into history. While the church is not itself the reign of God, the church continues Christ's task of proclaiming the reign, making it visible in history as we live out the Christ-life.

As we have seen before, this task involves us in spiritual warfare. Though soundly defeated through the death and resurrection of Jesus Christ, Satan has not yet run up the white flag of surrender. Until Christ consummates his lordship at his second coming, Satan will continue to wage war to maintain his dominion over earthly powers and principalities.

Some thirty years after the close of World War II, a lone Japanese soldier was found on an isolated Pacific island. He did not know that the war was ended; he did not know that his side had gone down in defeat. Those who found him offered him rescue from his solitary confinement; they sought to restore him to community; they brought him the news that the war had ended. Yet he couldn't believe it. He responded to their offers with a scowl and the muzzle of an old gun. Finally his rescuers persuaded him to go with them; thus he began the process of coming to grips with a new reality and of living a new life.

This is the situation we, as the body of Christ, find as we go out to rescue and restore those whom Satan has ensnared in his battle. They don't know their leader has been defeated. They put their scowls and their weapons between themselves and salvation. We know their delusion, because each one of us in the Lord's army was once an enemy of Christ. However, we also know the power of the truth and the excitement of coming to grips with the new reality of Christ's reign.

Because we love our leader, because we have seen what Christ has done in our own lives, and because we know that Christ reigns with justice and mercy, we put on the whole armor of God. We take upon ourselves the breastplate of righteousness, the helmet of salvation, and the shoes of peace. We take in our hands the shield of faith and the sword of the Spirit, and we march forth to reclaim lost lives and to reform fallen institutions. Because we are the body of ". . . Jesus Christ, who is the faithful witness, the firstborn from the dead, and the ruler of the kings of the earth" (Revelation 1:5), we march to our task with joy. We know that in our path we leave not devastation but *life*, for Christ's victory has brought liberation from the bondage of Satan's power. As his body, we bring healing, renewal, and hope.

To participate in this spiritual warfare, the church must function both as a fellowship of the strong and a hospital for the weak. While it is, therefore, legitimate for the church to focus on healing and comforting, too often this is allowed to become the major or sole focus.

". . . in the Bible," said Dr. Martin Lloyd-Jones in one of his sermons, "I find a barracks, not a hospital. It is not a doctor you need, but a Sergeant Major. Here we are on the parade ground slouching about. A doctor is no good; it is discipline we need. We need to listen to the Sergeant Major: 'Yield not to temptation, but yield to God.' That is the trouble with the church today; there is too much of the hospital element; we have lost sight of the great battle."[1]

How can we remain in our church pews nursing our cuts and scrapes while our foe mutilates the lives of millions of people? How can we keep the healing power of the Holy Spirit to ourselves when most of the pain lies outside the doors of the church? If our churches are more like hospitals, it is because we have tried to ignore the warfare. Our armor lies strewn at our feet while our enemy shoots his flaming arrows and we go running for bandages.

Some do put on their armor and march out of their hospital-churches, but they march out alone. They try to do battle single-handedly. These people deserve commendation for their willingness to respond to Christ's call, and yet they find themselves battered and weary. The war must be fought by the whole church, not just by isolated soldiers.

In many cases the church is at the forefront of the battle, waging war against the powers with evangelism and service projects. But when social-justice issues arise, the church backs away. Sometimes church people offer the rationale that individual Christians may get involved in such issues, but not the church. This separation of individuals from their community smacks strongly of Western individualism. The biblical picture shows the individual Christian and the corporate church body as inseparably intertwined in both existence and duty (Romans 12:4-5). The Christian finds his or her purpose and task in the Christian community, while the purpose of the Christian community is to enable, support, strengthen, and carry out the God-given purposes of the members of whom it is composed. Social justice is one of those God-given purposes, in league with evangelism and social service.

Others quote the Great Commission as a support for their argument that the church has no responsibility for social justice. "Therefore go and make disciples of all nations, baptizing them in the name of the Father and of the Son and of the Holy Spirit, and teaching them to obey everything I have commanded to you" (Matthew 28:19-20a). According to Jesus' words, the duty of the church is indeed evangelizing and equipping persons to be disciples. And teaching—teaching all that Jesus commanded his disciples. A careful reading of Scripture reveals a central emphasis upon love and justice in Jesus' mandates to his disciples. (See chapters 3 and 4.)

Still others who object to the church's involvement in social-justice issues point to the separation of church and state: the church should not meddle in issues of the state any more than the state should meddle in the affairs of the church. In reality, the principle of the separation of church and state preserves the independence of the church so that it can address and criticize the government on matters of justice affecting the populace, across religious lines. The separation prevents either the church or the state from using the other for narrow ends. A religious body does not receive a favored political position. It cannot enact legislation in the interest of only its people or its own concerns. In a democracy the church can function freely as one of the independent groups of society pressuring and petitioning the government for justice. The church will differ from most other interest groups in that its motives and purposes will be more altruistic, seeking the good of the powerless and oppressed rather than seeking favored status for its own selfish interests.

Yet, others object, if the church can get involved in social-justice issues, who will speak for the church on controversial subjects? What if there is disagreement over those issues within the church? How can we possibly risk making mistakes in Christ's name?

To address the last question first, we can respond that every day individual Christians risk making mistakes on issues of doctrine in Christ's name. Why should we be more concerned about making mistakes on social-justice issues than in these other areas? Are we pretending that the church is already so nearly perfect that we are afraid of tarnishing it?

Who speaks for the church, especially if there is disagreement? The church is a whole made up of many parts, and so the decision making of the church should mirror that fact. A statement or act should not be made in the name of the church as a whole unless it has been democratically arrived at and established by the church. A majority opinion should be sought because every Christian has access to the Holy Spirit for guidance in decision making. Yet unanimity is not necessary because all church bodies remain partly carnal, awaiting the perfection of the day of Christ. A dissenting minority should not prevent a church from taking a stance on a social-justice issue any more than it would on a doctrinal issue or on hiring staff. The church must weigh in the balance the need to strive for unity within the fellowship and the necessity of carrying out the commands of Christ.

The argument that the church should not be involved corporately in social issues can finally be put to rest by looking at the spiritual gifts with which the church is endowed for ministry. These gifts are given to individual Christians to advance the ministry of the church as a whole. Are there any which deal with social ministry? We find the gifts of giving to the poor (2 Corinthians 8:7), service, giving aid, acts of mercy, and leadership (Romans 12:7-8).

The body of Christ contributes to constructive social change in three ways: through the various forms of social action and service that it performs, through the impact of its witness, and through the support it gives to individuals involved in mission.

The church has often been at the forefront of the effort to meet needs and to make life better for suffering people. The example of Jesus Christ stimulates such a response. Direct intentional action—service, advocacy, material aid—has characterized the body of Christ on earth and must continue to do so until his return.*

In addition to direct, intentional action, the church contributes to social change through the impact of its witness. As Jesus put it, "You are the light of the world. A city on a hill cannot be hidden. Neither do people light a lamp and put it under a bowl. Instead they put it on its stand, and it gives light to everyone in the house. In the same way, let your light shine before [people], that they may see your good deeds and praise your Father in heaven" (Matthew 5:14-16).

The church should strive to embody the reign of God in its relationships, its values, its norms, and its life-style. It will differ radically from the outside world—not just in a narrow, pietistic sense, as in demanding that its members don't drink, dance, smoke, or go to movies— but rather in a deeper and broader sense that corresponds to the very attributes of God. God created the church, loves the church, and wants the church to represent God on earth. Church life should be characterized by love, mercy, justice, grace, forgiveness, holiness, righteousness, and truth, for these are characteristics of God and of God's reign.

In keeping with its nature, the church contributes to social change by withdrawing support from practices which run contrary to the inbreaking of the reign of God. A historic example is the northern churches' withdrawal of support from the system of slavery and their work at the forefront of the abolition movement. A current example is the number of churches going on record as opposing the build-up of nuclear weaponry.

At the same time that the church withdraws support from ungodly practices, it presents the alternative of a community that lives in obedience to God and in so doing creates whole persons. The church is the instrument that God uses to bring people to conversion; it is the social context of the believers' sanctification, the new realm of social existence in which we grow in the grace of Jesus Christ; and it is the launchpad for mission. While pointing out the shortcomings of contemporary society, the church offers an alternative reality created by God and reflecting God's wholeness. This adds credibility to the church's critique of society, simultaneously providing a context for the growth and support of the Christ-followers.

*Many churches have found that forming a "social-action" or "church-and-society" committee helps them to carry out their mission. Such a committee spearheads the work of educating the congregation about needs, problems, and issues; focuses the energy of the congregation to address areas of need and—insofar as that particular congregation is able—organizes appropriate action; and acts as liaison with community organizations and with social-action committees of other churches.

A person reportedly arrived at a church just as the members were leaving one Sunday morning. Making her way up to the pastor, the visitor queried, "I must be late; when does your service begin?" The pastor replied, "Our service begins at twelve; worship begins at eleven."

This pastor and church had their priorities right. The church should be a place of worship and renewal, a supportive base from which its members launch out into mission. Living out the life of God's reign is not easy in a society that is hostile to God. Society has powerful ways of foisting its values upon us, antithetical though they may be to the way of life God desires for us. As Paul exhorted Timothy, "Endure hardship with us like a good soldier of Christ Jesus. No one serving as a soldier gets involved in civilian affairs—he wants to please his commanding officer" (2 Timothy 2:3-4). The church is unequaled in the kind of support it can give to its members as they are involved in mission. We need to return to the church for a renewed sense of purpose, for renewed motivation, for unconditional and loving acceptance, for mutual support; in sum, we return to the church for a renewed awareness of the existence, character, and commands of the God we love and serve.

Moreover, the church supports the individual involved in mission in a unique way. It helps the individual to identify his or her spiritual gifts, assists in the development of those gifts, and affirms and supports the person in the use of those gifts.

God left the church on earth for a purpose. We are the front ranks of the reign of God, proclaiming Christ's victory over sin and death with might and valor. At the same time, we are the underground resistance effort; living in occupied territory, we refuse to cooperate with Satan, the prince of the power of the air. We do all we can do to undermine his dastardly plans.

We have experienced the healing of Christ. We must spring from our sickbeds, don our armor, and take our stand with him!

ENGAGE

The Church and the Civil Order

Refer to the case study on pages 72-74. Look at question 5 again and reread your recorded thoughts. After reading this chapter, would you respond any differently?

In a brief paragraph, sum up your views about the role of the church in seeking social justice.

Consider the following case study:

A young African pastor, prominent in the struggle for justice and freedom in Rhodesia, actively participated along with his family in the life of a [Protestant] congregation in Washington, D.C., for two years while he was doing additional study. When he returned to Rhodesia he was arrested without charges being brought, and there was fear for his ultimate safety. The pastor of the [Washington, D.C.] church assumed that the congregation would want to be among the first to voice its protest in appropriate channels to this imprisonment of a man they knew to represent moderate and principled Christian leadership much needed in his community. To the pastor's astonishment no body of the church would take any official action. They felt action should be left to individuals since not all members might want to participate in what would be a political protest. Of course, in the absence of courageous action by the congregational leadership few individuals took action either.[2]

1. If you were chairperson of a leadership body of this church, would you:

   a) suggest that the church take official action to protest the arrest of the Rhodesian pastor?

   b) recommend that action be left up to individuals?

2. On what grounds did you base your decision?

Decisions, Decisions

The time has come for your group to come to a consensus on some organizational matters.

1. Decision making:

   a) Will it be democratic?

   b) What will constitute a quorum?

   c) What will be needed to carry a vote—simple majority, ¾ majority, unanimity?

   d) Who will chair the meetings?

2. Selection of leaders:

   a) How will they be selected—nomination from the floor, nominating committee, volunteers?

   b) How will they be elected—ballot, voice vote?

   c) What offices will be necessary—chairperson, vice chairperson, secretary, treasurer, committee heads . . . ?*

   d) How long will terms run?

3. Differences of opinion:

   a) How can they be properly expressed and channeled so as to be most constructive?

   b) With whom will the buck stop concerning grievances, and how will conflicts be handled?

4. Discipline:

   a) Will there be an attendance requirement?

   b) What commitment must be made to the group?

   c) What procedure will be followed if assigned tasks are not completed?

You may want to divide into four groups and have each group discuss one of the four areas above. Each small group should return to the next meeting of the whole group with its recommendations for procedures in its assigned area. Then the group as a whole should discuss the recommendations, perhaps amend them, and vote on them, adopting the results as your group's by-laws. These should be typed and distributed to each group member.

What Is Your Church's "Social-Awareness Quotient"?

If your group belongs to the same church and the pastor is not a part of your group, you might want to schedule a meeting with your pastor in the near future to discuss his or her viewpoints on:

1. Major needs in the church and the community. (Your pastor is a good resource person in this area, because his or her job brings the pastor into contact with a broad variety of needs and problems inside and outside of the church. Your pastor can also help direct you to resources provided by your denomination, which can supply

---

*Remember to try matching spiritual gifts with the division of labor. For instance, often a person whose primary spiritual gift is "helps" would be miserable in a position of leadership. Persons with this gift generally prefer to be involved as support workers. And in the formation of your committees, don't forget to include the responsibilities of coordinating worship activities, public relations, research, community relations, etc.

you with more information on the background and addressing of certain needs.)

2. Evangelism and social action, as they fit into the mission of your church. (Your pastor has been gifted by God to equip and enable your church for ministry; his or her opinion on strategy in your church and community is valuable. Also, it is vital that you strive to fit your action into the total ministry of your church.)

3. The existence and/or function of a social-action committee in your church. If there is one, you should consult with it and work in cooperation with it. If there is not one, your group might consider offering to serve in that capacity. This would require a willingness to submit to and be accountable to the leadership of your church. Working under the auspices of a local church gives your group a broader base of support and resources than you would have on your own, but it also may narrow the choice of issues you can address because you need to seek the approval of your congregation and/or its leaders.

If your group consists of members from several churches, you will be acting as an ecumenical and/or parachurch group. Your group members can serve as resource persons to the pastors and social-action committees of your churches and vice versa. If the churches can agree to support your group in working on the issue(s) and need(s) that you choose to work on, you will have a broad base of community support.

Either way, be prepared for some frustration. There is often quite a gap between the ideal of how a church should be involved in working toward social justice, and the reality of how much energy and resources it has left after dealing with routine "maintenance" issues. Don't expect your excitement and commitment to be automatically contagious. Continue to love your church and "handle with prayer."

Deciding Upon a Manageable Issue

During the next week, be thinking about what need and/or issue your group might like to act together to address and what kind of action that might require. Think back on your past meetings, discussions, and answers to previous "Engage" exercises. Prayerfully consider the possibilities, and expect God's Holy Spirit to guide you not only individually but also as a group.

8

Politics as a Path to Justice

Democratic government grants Christians the right publicly to criticize, review, debate, and challenge current procedures and policies. Under those conditions, the message of Romans 13 imposes on them the duty to make use of that right.[1]

One of the authors, who teaches an adult Sunday school class, once asked the class members the question "If humans had never sinned, would we still have a govenment?" A good deal of discussion ensued. We finally concluded that we would still need governments to take care of our needs for organization and order. However, there would be no need for the government to exercise its policing function.

As we pondered the question, we enjoyed imagining a world in which there was no sin, in which every person upheld the rights of all other persons. Unfortunately, real life presents another world, one tainted with sin. What is the role of government, in God's plan, in a fallen world? And what should be the Christian's relationship to the government?

A classic passage outlining the role of the state in God's scheme of things, Romans 13 characterizes the ruler as "an agent of wrath to bring punishment on the wrongdoer . . . the authorities are God's servants, who give their full time to governing" (Romans 13:4-6). While some on the contemporary American scene see government primarily as a threat to freedom, God's order regards government as primarily a threat to wrongdoers. Indeed, Romans 13 could be summed up: "Overcome evil with good; abstain from evil so that you will have no fear of the governing powers, which are ordered by God; cooperate with governing authorities in doing good and in paying taxes; render to all of them their due."

Though part of God's plan for maintaining justice and order, governments themselves bear the taint of humankind's sinfulness. They are the scene of the struggle between the fallen worldly powers and the authority of God for the control of the human community. The citizens of God's reign must join in the struggle with the twin goals of fighting *for* God's intention of what human government and society should be and *against* the corruption to which humans and their institutions are vulnerable.

As citizens of a democracy, we find this responsibility doubled, for we *are* the government. Ideally, we each have a voice in our governance—electing our leaders and representatives, expressing our views on issues and administrative concerns, having a say about how much we are taxed and for what purposes tax revenues are used, drafting and supporting legislation which upholds justice for all.

This necessarily involves each of us in the political process, the nuts-and-bolts process that makes our government run. Different people choose to be involved at different levels. For the majority, involvement extends primarily to the voting booth and letters of support and concern to congressional representatives. Some people participate in the political process at the local level, running for elective office or seeking appointment to public office. Others run for state or national offices, while some participate in the political process behind the scenes as lobbyists for companies or citizens' organizations.

Surely you have heard someone say, "We don't talk religion or politics. That's why we still get along." Politics in a democratic society is by nature controversial. The pluralism of peoples and interests results in competition for political advantage, for pieces of the budgetary pie, for protection, for opportunity, for power. Sometimes what is best for the many is also best for the few, and vice versa. At other times, however, there is intense struggle. Political decision making involves determining what is the best decision for the majority without obstructing justice for each minority group. Political decision making involves power—its use, its assessment, its distribution. Sometimes that power is wielded to implement a good, sometimes to restrain an evil, and sometimes that power is misused for the politician's or the state's own selfish ends.

These realities of the political system—this use and potential abuse of power—cause some Christians to argue that Christians should not be involved in the political process. They feel that we are under a higher ethical standard which is incompatible with such involvement. They will often quote Mark 10:42-43 to support their argument.

Jesus called them together and said, "You know that those who are regarded as rulers of the Gentiles lord it over them, and their high officials exercise authority over them. Not so with you. Instead, whoever wants to become great among you must be your servant. . . ."

Using this passage to proscribe any political involvement, however, mistakes its main thrust. Rather than telling his disciples to stay out of leadership roles or political involvement, Jesus was warning them of the temptation facing those in such roles to misuse their power for personal elevation. Jesus' words about the Gentile rulers show them to be characterized by hierarchy, by status, and by status-seeking. This ranking and one-upmanship have no place in God's reign; rather, among God's people, leadership must be characterized by servanthood.

Mark Hatfield, a committed Christian and a United States Senator, fleshed out Jesus' words when he described his experience as a Christian politician:

> Radical allegiance to Jesus Christ transforms one's entire perspective on political reality. Priorities become totally changed; a whole new understanding of what is truly important bursts forth. There is an uncompromised identification with the needs of the poor and the oppressed. One is placed in fundamental opposition to structures of injustice and forms of national idolatry. Further, there is a commitment to the power of love as the only means to the end. We are to empty ourselves as he did for the sake of others.
>
> Reconciling such a commitment with daily demands, pressures, and expectations of political life creates constant tension. The temptations and subtle seductions of the world's system of thought exercise a constant power over anyone in the political realm. My own journey has repeatedly revealed the forceful pressures that would conform me to the world's values, keeping me from being transformed, as St. Paul puts it, by the renewing of the Spirit.[2]

On one hand, Christians are motivated by God's grace to work for "justice in the gate" (Amos 5:15, RSV). In so doing, however, they live in an atmosphere replete with the temptations of power and worldly success. Living in this tension is not easy; Senator Hatfield entitled his book *Between a Rock and a Hard Place* to characterize his experience. Nevertheless, the tensions of political involvement do not negate it as an important path to justice. In fact, the other paths to justice—evangelism, the witness and work of Christian community, strategic non-cooperation, and even revolution—find their completion in legislation. Legislation crystallizes desired social change, making its demands clear, concrete, and enforceable.

Soon another question must arise for the Christian involved in the political process. Should one attempt to coerce people to live according to Christian values? This question has often arisen stated in more general terms: Can you legislate morality?

Christians are not naive about human nature. Evidence from Scripture and from history makes us aware that people simply are not good enough to ensure that injustice can be controlled voluntarily. There is and always has been the necessity of external constraint. This external constraint takes the form of enforceable laws that protect the rights of each individual and of society-at-large. So we see that the objective aspect of morality—how people actually treat one another—*can* be regulated. In fact, the great majority of our laws are aimed at controlling behavior.

However, morality has another aspect, the subjective aspect, which cannot be regulated. You cannot force someone to love or respect another person. Nevertheless, while attitudes greatly affect one's behavior, in matters of law and justice it is behavior that matters. Harvey Cox brought this out in *The Secular City.*

> The recent civil rights revolution in America has proved at least one thing: Negroes are not so much interested in winning whites to a less prejudiced attitude as they are in preventing them from enforcing the prejudice they do have. The Negro revolt is not aimed at winning friends but at winning freedom, not interpersonal warmth but institutional justice. . . . The inmates of the urban concentration camp do not long for fraternization with the guards; what they want is the abolition of the prison; not improved relations with the captors but "release from captivity."[3]

Law does have an educating and conditioning effect that can affect the subjective aspect of morality. One's attitudes often change in order to achieve a better balance with one's behavior. Changes of this nature have been observed in the South, where whites' attitudes regarding relations with blacks have become less prejudiced in the years following enforced desegregation of schools, housing, and other areas of public life.

Having discerned between subjective and objective morality in regard to their openness to regulation, we must nonetheless conclude that not all matters of right are appropriate for legislation. There are matters that should be left to private discretion as long as they do not injure the well-being of another person or of the community as a whole. In addition, legislation should not be used to obtain special advantage for a private group within society.

This does not mean that groups with strong, distinctive convictions must give these up in order to participate in the political process. On the contrary, if all citizens in a democracy reduced their beliefs to the lowest common denominator, the system would work for no one. Democracy depends upon pluralism, upon people working in the political system on the basis of their own convictions, whether or not they are in the majority.

Much of politics concerns the question of "Which morality?" Christians must uphold their distinctive set of values as a viable model in the political decision-making process. Rather than imposing the values of a minority upon the rest of society, Christians involved in the political process must seek support for their proposed regulations and programs from other groups in society. Coalition and cooperation are integral parts of the democratic process. Often, there will be groups who share the Christian vision of justice—albeit from a secular standpoint—for though our society is not Christian, it has been strongly influenced throughout its history by Christian principles and example.

We must beware, at this point, of the type of political involvement seen in the "Moral Majority" and similar organizations. Far from seeking justice as both the goal and the means, the new Christian right pushes to foist a minority morality upon the larger society, portraying what they are doing as a divine agenda. Such groups neglect pluralism and seek to work through "moral" influence, antagonism, and recruitment of broad support by equating their political agenda with religious devotion.

The new Christian right features an unfortunate coupling of conservative Christianity with conservative politics. The latter is characterized by an attitude of "the less government involvement, the better." The goal of such a political perspective is economic freedom, not economic justice.

The involvement of the new Christian right in this kind of politics is rationalized via the God-and-country "sacraments" of the American civil religion. These politics are seen as the historic ones which made this country great; they are considered ordained of God and are seen as God's will for America today. Those persons who champion the new Christian right pose as God's humble servants, seeking to restore God's will and once again to make this country great. Some issues on which they speak out do involve matters of moral consequence. However, they neglect the moral consequences of the economic agenda which they vigorously promote. Though professing a profound belief in Scripture and its mandates, they exhibit a profound naiveté concerning the greedy drive of unrestrained human nature and concerning God's commands to seek economic and social justice.[4]

Despite the central importance of working through the political process in order to achieve social change, the church must beware of relying too heavily upon political and economic means to deal with social evil. Our call and our mission go broader and deeper than the political process ever could.

Further, law that is effective, enforceable, and sustains respect can rise little above the general sense of right and wrong. Morality depends as much on teaching as it does on enforcement of law, and morality cannot be taught to a society without religion.[5] The law needs the church.

The body of Christ has the responsibility of developing and nurturing moral and ethical values in society which will support and respond to God's call to justice and righteousness. Since effective law is tied to the general level of morality, the church must prepare for just laws by raising the general level of morality through its teaching and example.

Laws can control external behavior but cannot create in persons the desire to uphold the rights of others and to seek their welfare. Through its witness and acts of ministry, the church—empowered and enabled by the Holy Spirit—touches and shapes the subjective morality of people. The teachings of Christ and the indwelling of the Holy Spirit create in people those qualities that are necessary for legislated justice to be sustained: self-respect, self-acceptance, tolerance, mutual respect, honesty, a sense of right and duty, a desire for equal treatment for all, fidelity to law, and care that seeking one's own profit and well-being does not injure others. Without the presence of "new creatures in Christ," our society would be morally bankrupt, incapable of a vision of true justice and lacking the means to implement it.

The church needs to be active on both fronts, in the political arena and in the larger society, striving for social righteousness in all aspects of its mission. We are to be leavening agents that permeate all of life with the presence and promise of God's reign.

This leavening must affect the type of political reform we seek as agents of God's reign. We cannot wholeheartedly endorse any political system. God's Word and Spirit give us a perspective on human institutions that aids us in assessing realistically the strengths and weaknesses of any system. We can then focus our efforts on constructive criticism and efforts to bring about positive change.

Too much of the reform that has been sought in the history of our nation has been a "co-optable" type of reform. Reformers responded to surface problems, rather than delving into the structural problems behind these surface problems. The reforms they proposed, while improvements, have made little impact on the total functioning of the system.

Consider the regulating commissions, such as the Nuclear Regulatory Commission, which were set up as reform measures to watchdog specific segments of business and public service. Reformers, concerned about the possible excesses of business in a free capitalistic society, worked hard to set up commissions to regulate such business practices as price-fixing monopolies. These commissions, established by Congress and administered by the executive branch of government, were to represent and protect the interests of the people as consumers, workers, and taxpayers.

The watchdogs, however, soon became lapdogs. As both government and reformers, pleased with their success, turned their attention to other matters, the commissions functioned less as public agents policing businesses than as managers and advocates acting *for* the businesses. The industries to be regulated had a major say in who would sit on the commissions, and of course they chose their own representatives. This intimacy between the commissions and the industries abrogated any true representation of the public interest.

Despite the good intentions behind these reforms, the reformers did not go far enough in assessing the roots of the problems. Hence the "cure" did little more than disguise the symptoms. The reform was co-opted by those it was intended to restrain.

The "Great Society" programs of the 1960s provide another example of "co-optable" reform. These programs focused on alleviating the symptoms of social and economic injustice rather than on addressing the sources of injustice in our political and economic system. Welfare and job programs were set up, but they were mainly paternalistic, Band-Aid remedies. There was no real sharing of power or of opportunity. Reformers and protesters settled for symbolic success rather than pursuing fundamental changes that would have ensured long-lasting reform.

In contrast to this "co-optable" type of reform, we must seek creative reforms which directly address the roots of our social and systemic ills. The vision for this reform comes, of course, from the reign of God. While we realize that we cannot legislate the reign into being, it provides the goal and the guidelines for our work in history. This type of reform upsets the status quo, because it aims to modify unjust power relationships. It sets forth a new order of priorities, and it provides new models of how human life might be ordered.

While holding the vision of the reign before us, we bear no illusions about the possibility of readily accomplishing far-reaching political reform. We have to deal with the reality of the level of morality at hand. Therefore, we take a piecemeal approach, working toward fundamental change through a cumulative series of partial steps. We focus upon identifiable, concrete problems of justice that can be dealt with now. Each small victory is important because it advances us toward our goal.

Yet we don't expect our victories to sustain themselves; we keep watch lest our gains be co-opted, revoked, or altered out of recognition. Unlike the reformers who turned from their victories to other matters only to find their victories distorted and lost, we must remain vigilant. We must recognize that follow-up is as vital a part of our duty as the original efforts to launch a reform.

The denominations to which the authors belong have offices in Washington, D.C., which help their members to work for creative reform based on their Christian convictions. The American Baptist Churches in the U.S.A. has its Office of Governmental Relations. Those who staff the office work to represent the justice concerns of the denomination's membership to elected officials in Washington. They also help the membership to participate directly in creative political reform by keeping them informed of pertinent issues and events. As part of its ministry, the Board of Church and Society of the United Methodist Church performs similar functions as well as publishing a periodical entitled *Engage/Social Action*. Several other denominations also provide such service.

Bread for the World exemplifies another type of Christian organization pursuing creative reform, the public pressure group. Bread for the World's vision of God's justice in the production and distribution of food clashes with the present world order in which millions go hungry while the wealthy enjoy every possible luxury. They focus their efforts for reform upon the governmental decision-making structure that develops our food production and distribution policy. They lobby for increased foreign aid composed of greater percentages of food aid than military aid and directed to the poorest of the poor. They seek greater distributive justice, one law at a time.

Bread for the World monitors the outcomes of their legislative victories, making sure that the implementation reflects the intent of the law. They build upon past successes, working toward an ever-more-just system of distribution. They accept and learn from defeat, understanding that justice will never be completely realized in human government.

As we strive to be the whole people of God in a democratic society, we must proclaim God's reign in the corridors of power. We must not allow that to be our all-consuming mission, however, neglecting the other facets of our proclamation. Finally, we must remember that

> our call is to faithfulness, not to efficacy; it is to servanthood rather than power. We know that the most decisive action that we can take to shape history is to follow the way of Christ, to give ourselves to the building of the Body, and to pour out ourselves as he did in love.[6]

ENGAGE

A Tale of Two Senators

Does the fact that a politician professes to be a Christian necessarily mean that his or her practice of politics will be "Christian"—that it will clearly reflect the values and demands of the reign of God? Consider the perspectives and styles of two senators, both professing Christians and both of the same political party.

Senator Jesse Helms gives public testimony to his spiritual rebirth. His faithful attendance at church and his teaching of Sunday school have been noted in news magazines. A scion of conservative politics, he enjoys the backing of the "Moral Majority" and other conservative religious and political groups.

Senator Mark Hatfield also gives public testimony to his spiritual rebirth. He is an active church member and serves on the boards of several Christian organizations. A committed participant in the prayer-breakfast movement, Senator Hatfield is known for calling the nation to a "National Day of Humiliation, Fasting, and Prayer" on April 30, 1974.

Each of these men believe that their Christian faith has relevance to their political practice, and yet we find that they give it expression in quite different ways. Senator Helms emphasizes the responsibility and freedom of the individual; Senator Hatfield emphasizes the social responsibility of Christians and of our nation. These two different approaches lead to different conclusions regarding social issues.

In keeping with his perspective, Senator Helms opposes "big government." As chairman of the Senate Committee on Agriculture, Nutrition, and Forestry, he is in a position of power to influence programs that would grant food aid to the needy. However, Senator Helms's voting record shows that he has consistently opposed such programs.[7] (At the same time, he has actively lobbied and voted to continue generous federal subsidies to tobacco growers in his state.)

In another example of his opposition to government intervention, Senator Helms carried on a filibuster opposing renewal of the Voting Rights Act, the act that ensures equal access to the polls by all people of all races but that requires federal government involvement to do so. Senator Helms's belief in the rights of the individual has led him to the forefront of the effort to outlaw abortion and the effort to allow voluntary prayer in public schools.

Acting in accord with his convictions about social responsibility, Senator Hatfield has sponsored and actively supports legislation aimed at resolving the problem of world hunger, both domestic programs and foreign aid programs.[8] A veteran of World War II, he openly opposed the involvement of the United States in Vietnam, despite the risk such a position posed for his political future. He has cosponsored an amendment calling for a bilateral freeze on the production, deployment, and testing of nuclear weapons. He also has expressed a concern that our nation move toward a more careful stewardship of natural resources, particularly energy resources.[9]

Given these very brief synopses of the backgrounds and political stances of each senator, consider the following questions.

1. Of these two approaches toward giving expression to one's faith in political practice, with which do you find yourself more comfortable? Why?

2. Do you feel that either of these approaches more nearly fulfills the biblical call to seek "justice in the gate?" Which? Why?

3. If these men were pitted against each other in a senatorial race, for whom would you vote and why?

4. Does the fact that a politician professes to be a Christian necessarily mean that his or her practice of politics will reflect the values and demands of the reign of God?

5. If a politician professing to be a Christian and holding views similar to those of Senator Helms were pitted in a political race against a politician who did not claim to be a Christian but whose platform approached the demands of biblical justice, for whom would you vote? Why?

6. If a politician professing to be a Christian and holding views similar to those of Senator Hatfield were pitted in a political race against a politician who did not claim to be a Christian but whose platform approached the demands of biblical jusice, for whom would you vote? Why?

Legislating Morality?

For each act listed below, write yes or no in the proper columns in answer to the following questions:
1. Could this act legitimately be prohibited through legislation?
2. Could such a law be enforced effectively?

ACT	Could legitimately be prohibited through legislation	Could effectively be enforced
1. Getting drunk in one's own home		
2. Getting drunk on the highway		
3. Going to bed with another person's spouse		
4. Worshiping a false god		
5. Buying or selling pornographic literature		
6. Paying wages below the poverty level		
7. Renting out substandard housing		
8. Using government funds to support religious professionals		
9. Denouncing the U.S. government		
10. Refusing to pay income taxes		
11. Mutilating an animal		
12. Killing at the request of the victim		

Finalizing Decisions

Your group should now discuss and vote on the conclusions and recommendations resulting from your study of organizational matters. (See the section "Decisions, Decisions" on page 83.)

Focusing on a Manageable Issue

What is a "manageable issue?" It is an issue that your group has the ability, resources, experience, commitment, and desire to address with a likelihood of success. It is an issue on which everyone in your group can work and feel a sense of accomplishment without feeling constantly overwhelmed. In order to feel accomplishment, you must believe that your work is meeting a need. In order to keep from being overwhelmed, you must choose an issue within the scope of your group's power, so that you will not program yourselves for defeat.

Brainstorming (group exercise)

The object of this exercise is to compose a list of issues that your group might address. In brainstorming, people call out their ideas fast and furious. There is no discussion, no criticism, and no evaluation. The more creatively and boundlessly people think, the better the results of the brainstorming session.

Choose one member of your group to record all the suggestions on the blackboard, overhead projector transparency, or newsprint. You may want to set a time limit of ten or fifteen minutes.

Set your imagination free, but at the same time keep in mind the immediate context in which you will be working. Remember to include the possibilities that came up in past sessions, in your reading and thinking, and in your discussion with your pastor and church social action committee.

Establishing Priorities (individual exercise)

Once you have a list, keep it in a prominent place where everyone can see it. Each group member should now choose the five areas in which he or she feels the group is best suited and most committed to work. In choosing these five areas, remember to consider the resources of your group, the weekly time commitment of members, the length of commitment of members, the interests of group members, the needs of the church and community, your group's experience in social action, other groups in the community which may or may not be addressing the issue, and so forth.

After you have selected your top five areas, assign them ranks. Your highest priority is "1"; your next highest priority is "2"; and so on.

Amalgamating (group exercise)

Each person in the group should share his or her top five priorities, giving the rank she or he assigned to each. Your recording person should make a note of the numerical rank next to each stated area.

Once everyone has shared priorities, add up the total numbers assigned to each area. The lower the total for a given area, the greater the composite priority assigned to that area by your group. Determine in this way the top three priorities of your entire group.

Researching

Between now and your next meeting, you should research each of these three areas as thoroughly as possible. The most efficient way would be to divide into three study groups, with each group researching one area in depth. Your research sources will include books, magazines, newspapers, people "in-the-know" (experts and people close to those who have been hurt because of social problems), and organizations— whoever or whatever might help you derive information on your topic. Each of the three groups should divide among their members the burden of the research, determining:

1. what information we need;
2. where we can obtain that information;
3. who will research each area and when;
4. when we can get together to put our findings together.

The findings of each study group should be written up briefly and clearly and reproduced for each member of the entire group.

Your research should provide information on as many as possible of the following areas:

● How does this problem cause suffering?
● What is the root cause of this problem?
● What is the historical background of this problem? How did it develop? How has it been perpetuated? What solutions have been tried in the past, and how have they fared?
● What are some specific issues, within this general problem area, which our group could address?
● What other groups in our community (or at other levels) are working to address this problem and in what ways?
● What kinds of support are there for working on this problem— monetary support, moral support, political support, support of other involved groups or of other uninvolved groups?
● What does the Bible have to say about this problem area—its source, symptoms, or solution?
● How would our Christian convictions, illuminated by God's Word and guided by the Spirit, lead us to respond to this problem?

The information you gather should guide you as you select a manageable issue to address as a group. It should begin to enlighten you in your decision-making process as you consider the following questions:

1. Where is the need the greatest?
2. What are we most interested in and/or most desirous of addressing?
3. What lies within our power to address with a goodly measure of

success? (Success isn't everything, but it is pretty important to a fledgling group.) Do we have a probable chance of making a real difference? If we can't anticipate certain success, will our action nevertheless present a clear Christian witness?

4. If you are a church group, what best fits into the total ministry of our church? That is, what either works well with other programs or fills a big gap in the programming?

9

The Vital Role
of Citizens' Groups

(Before beginning to read this chapter, turn to the "Engage" section on page 108 and fill out the "Group-Involvement Inventory.")

How many times have you heard someone say, "I know things are bad, and something ought to be done. But what can just one person do?" Perhaps you've said it yourself.

A series of statements lies behind that question. I am powerless. There are situations and practices in our society which upset and concern me. I am aware of wrongs that ought not to go on. *Someone* should do something! Someone else, that is, not me. I'm concerned, but I doubt if I could make a difference. The wrongs are too big for me to face alone.

For most of us this is probably a realistic assessment. On our own we probably couldn't have a very great effect on correcting social evils. But why do we think that we have to confront them on our own? Perhaps we really don't want to respond. Or perhaps we have forgotten or ignored a central fact of social reality: the importance of groups.

In addition to individuals, groups are the building blocks that make up society. Everyone in society, except perhaps extreme recluses, belongs to one or more groups. Consider your own participation in groups, which you noted in the "Group-Involvement Inventory."

Groups play an essential role in society, because they integrate persons into the larger social fabric in a meaningful way. For each of us the statement "I am a member of society" does not carry nearly as much meaning as "I am a member of (*some specific group*)." We need the face to face contacts with other people that our group involvement provides. We need the sense of belonging, of participating, of knowing others, and of being known. It is in our group involvements that we come to know ourselves better as persons—who we are, what we can do, and what we like to do. It is also in our group involvements that we come to know better the society in which we live—what needs to be done, what we are allowed to do, and how it should be done.

Most of the groups to which we belong are voluntary associations. We belong to them because we choose to belong. Whereas we are born into a family group, we choose to be involved in church groups, social groups, political groups, etc.

Groups play an important role in the control of society. Every group has norms, which it expects its members to follow, and most groups have ways of enforcing proper behavior. Our society as a whole is controlled by groups, particularly the legal institutions that we call "government." Further, those holding official authority are influenced by special interest groups representing different segments of our society. So when a person laments, "What can I do? I'm just one individual," a good response to consider is "Join a citizens' group!"

For a democratic form of government to function, two things are necessary: (1) the facts pertaining to public decision must reach the citizens in an understandable form; and (2) the citizens' opinions on the facts must be translated into government acts.[1] This is a two-way flow: information flowing to the citizens and responses flowing from the citizens.

How well has this two-way flow worked in your own experience? First, consider information flowing to the citizens. Have you ever walked into the voting booth and discovered that you've never heard of many of the names on the ballot? Have you ever had to vote on a public referendum but felt that you really weren't informed about the issues involved?

Suppose that you knew all the names on the ballot and that you felt you had a handle on the issues involved in the referendum. Where did you get your information? From the newspaper? TV, maybe? Can you be sure the reporting was fair and unbiased? Can you be sure that the media gave all the candidates a fair chance, that they covered all the issues involved in the referendum? One of the authors lives in a county in which the major newspapers and local radio stations are owned by one family. It is generally known that their pet interests receive a measure of editorial privilege. Could that affect the democratic process?

Hmmm. What does all this say about that important flow of information to the citizens? Unless we have unlimited time to conduct our own research into local, state, and federal issues, we find that we are uninformed. Or, we find ourselves very dependent upon other sources for our information, some of which may be biased or based on value systems very different from ours.

If this vital flow has broken down, how can the flow of response from each citizen possibly hold up in any meaningful way? Lack of information can result in bad decisions or no decisions at all!

Here we see the importance of voluntary associations such as citizens' groups. Many such organizations gather their own information, independent of the news media. They can support technicians, scholars, and researchers with special expertise beyond that of the average citizen, who glean necessary information and share it with group members in a way that enables them to make informed decisions. These groups also aid in the flow of response from the citizens to the government—keeping members informed about when key decisions are coming up, who should be contacted, and also providing the information they need to make an informed response.

Such organizations are vital for the functioning of democracy at every level of government—local, state, and national. By banding together to support such groups, individuals in cooperation can accomplish much more than anyone alone possibly could.

One would think that with the advancements in communications and transportation that our country has experienced, citizen participation in public affairs would be at an all-time high. Unfortunately, the reverse holds true. In 1892, 87 percent of all eligible voters participated in presidential elections; in the 1960s, only 57 percent participated; in the 1980 presidential election, only 52.4 percent of eligible voters participated.[2] These figures indicate a clear trend toward less participation in the political decision-making process.

This trend holds true among church members as well. For the most part, our churches have emphasized the inner faith and family life of individuals rather than the relevance of our faith in the larger community. Further, the demands that church activities place on members' time leave little time for participation in other voluntary associations. Nonetheless, churches should encourage the participation of their members in citizens' groups as a necessary extension of the churches' mission.

Voluntary associations can be divided into three types: 1) collectivities "in themselves," 2) collectivities "for themselves," and 3) collectivities "for the public." The activities of the first type of voluntary association are concerned only with the interactions of the group and what that does for its members. They have no purpose that extends beyond the confines of the group itself. An example would be a weight-watching group or a square-dancing group. The second type of voluntary association works in the greater community for the interests of that particular group. An example would be athletic-team- or band-boosters groups. The third type of voluntary association works for other groups or for a shared interest of the community as a whole. An example would be a citizens' group.

For the Christian, should membership in any one type of group be favored above another? Given the constraints of time and energy which most of us face, yes, we must choose involvement in that type of group which does the most to advance the reign of our Lord. The third type of group, collectivities "for the public," goes furthest in allowing us to put some clout behind our convictions concerning social justice.

The quote at the beginning of chapter 8 bears repeating here:

> Democratic government grants Christians the right publicly to criticize, review, debate, and challenge current procedures and policies. Under those conditions, the message of Romans 13 imposes on them the duty to make use of that right.[3]

If we find ourselves neglecting that duty due to our involvement in more self-oriented types of groups or due to total lack of involvement in any group, we should consider changing our patterns of involvement so as to use our time and energy more effectively in Christ's service.

God's followers are called to be people of justice. If we do not involve ourselves in public decison making, most decisions will be made by groups representing special, selfish interests. Consider the following example.

Richard Barringer, conservation commissioner of the state of Maine, believed that his office should represent the public interest in caring for the vast tracts of northern forests owned by lumber companies. This came as a novel idea, for as we discussed in the last chapter, commissions have largely been more sensitive to industry than to the public interest they were intended to represent.

Mr. Barringer acted upon his concern for the public interest by adding an amendment to legislation dealing with a budworm epidemic. His amendment called for the lumber companies to assume the costs for the spraying of the forests, with the state chipping in only in proportion to its expected income from taxes, recreation fees, and leasing of public lands. The amendment also provided tax incentives to the lumber companies for improving the forest with types of trees less susceptible to the budworm attack.

According to both government and industry sources, his amendment was the first forestry bill in anyone's memory to be introduced without the prior approval of the landowners. "This just isn't the way it works," lamented the executive director of the Maine Forest Products Council.[4] Given the biblical call to seek justice, we dare not neglect involvement in democratic decision making. While few of us occupy positions of power like that of Mr. Barringer, we can wield similar influence by pooling our power as voting, tax-paying citizens with others of similar convictions. We should consider involving ourselves in groups that seek to overcome social evils, that function for the sake of underprivileged groups, and that give allegiance and substance to prophetic protest.

Citizens' groups advocate policies for the general welfare, in contrast to groups which seek the vested interests of a privileged minority.* Citizens' groups work separately from the structure of political parties, serving their members and the public in general through their investigation of social and political conditions and through exposure of injustice.

Citizens' groups recommend policy and exert pressure for passage of needed proposals by raising citizen awareness and mobilizing support. Once desired laws have been enacted, citizens' groups perform a monitoring function: they exert pressure for the enforcement of these laws, even to the point of litigation. In this way they work toward creative reform, and protect their reforms from being co-opted.

Human rights and environmental groups give a great deal of their time to press the government to enforce the law. In the face of the great industrial influence upon the Nuclear Regulatory Commission, groups like the Union of Concerned Scientists have been doing what the federal government should have been doing all along: watchdogging nuclear power. Such groups frequently resort to litigation to bring about enforcement of the law or to bring about new judicial precedent in the courts.

In terms of effectiveness in influencing public policy, it is better to support and be involved in groups which are *not* tax exempt. Whereas tax-exempt groups cannot lobby government leaders, groups which are not tax exempt can be much more directly involved in the political process. By being involved with these groups, individuals can multiply their impact. One's voice becomes part of a group rather than a lone voice. An example of the effectiveness of such a group is a national law firm for Native Americans, the Native American Rights Fund.

*The authors acknowledge that the term *citizens' group* can also be used to refer to groups of citizens that seek a twisted form of what they consider to be the general welfare, for instance the Ku Klux Klan, neo-Nazis, etc. Nevertheless, as used in this book the term *citizens' group* refers to those groups dedicated to seeking ends in line with biblical justice and wholeness. (Even those ends can be open to a wide variety of interpretation, but such is our freedom in a democracy and our responsibility as citizens of God's reign.)

Fundamental to the treaties with the Native Americans was the agreement by the United States to protect the tribes in their rights. The federal trust responsibility was delegated to the Secretary of the Interior, whose instrument of authority has been the Bureau of Indian Affairs. There, the tribes believe, the trust relationship has been grossly violated, as have the nation's obligations as trustee outside of the Federal courts.

The wave of Native American litigation that has swept into the courts since the mid-sixties is a result of the existence of trained Native American lawyers under the support of groups like the Native American Rights Fund. In the past decade the number of lawyers working almost exclusively on Native-American-related matters tripled from no more than three dozen to nearly one hundred, and half of these lawyers were themselves Native Americans. The result has been access to lawyers and the courts for Native Americans and their tribes, which is unprecedented in their experience.

The matters covered involve a panorama of Native American concerns, and the stakes are particularly great in cases concerning the use and ownership of land. Here, either in land or its monetary equivalent, there is opportunity to deal with the basis of poverty: the lack of power. Support for the Native American Rights Fund has an impact in terms of justice which cannot easily be matched in equivalent direct relief.

Financial involvement in these organizations is vital to their success and should not be slighted. Nevertheless, money should not be given as an "easy out" in place of giving one's time and energy. A suggested principle would be to contribute for those activities that you cannot do yourself rather than for those activities that you *can* do.

Contributing to a pressure group not only supports effective lobbying activities but also procures technology and resources. Members benefit from the information-gathering and expert analysis of the pressure group's staff. They are aided in performing their duties as citizens, for they are made aware of important issues and are enabled to make informed decisions. Thus, contributing to pressure groups can be an effective method of giving to the poor in a way which does not directly treat the symptoms—though that is also necessary—but which works at the root causes of those symptoms in the power structure.

Some citizens' pressure groups are mainly organized at the local level, such as neighborhood organizations. Some of these local groups, finding that the issues which concern them also concern others beyond their communities, grow to become national and regional in their concerns. Massachusetts Fair Share is one such organization which developed in this way.

One of the authors participates in a citizens' group organized at the local level for the purpose of learning about and acting on issues of nuclear war and peace. While not affiliated with any one larger organization, this group receives information from such sources as denominational agencies of its members and the American Friends Service Committee. The group meets once a month for two hours. One third of that time centers upon worship through devotions and music. One third of the time has an educational focus—members presenting research they have done, guest speakers, discussion of literature, etc. The last third of the meeting is devoted to business matters and planning for various group activities. Through their involvement in the group, members keep informed about proposed and pending legislation in their area of concern. They also work together to raise awareness in the community about nuclear armament issues through such activities as staffing a booth at the county fair, staging skits, sponsoring a speakers bureau, and so forth. The time and energy that each member invests in the group produces a great return in terms of the service and accomplishment of the group as a whole.

Some groups originally developed at the national level but work hard to involve citizens and to develop organizations at the local level. Bread for the World has a strong organization that lobbies at the national level. This group nonetheless depends upon the participation of individual citizens and has developed an efficient network for involving members in local and congressional-district groups which maintain a vital communications flow with the organization at the national level. It also features the opportunity for churches to become involved through its Covenant Church Program.

Amnesty International is another organization that strongly encourages local group involvement. A widely respected and broadly supported organization working for the release of individuals across the world who are imprisoned or tortured for political reasons, Amnesty International provides direct ways in which its members can be involved beyond making financial contributions. Its local groups "adopt" prisoners and concentrate their energies on letter-writing and contacting the government officials who wield influence in the case involved. They write to embassies, to the press, to the prisoner, and to the prisoner's family.

Participating in public pressure groups, such as the ones mentioned or the myriad of others* covering almost every significant social issue,

*The *Encyclopedia of Associations*, 3 vols., ed. Denise S. Akey, (Detroit: Gale Research Co., 1981), 16th ed., can be found in most libraries. Volume 1 lists "National Organizations of the United States"; Volume 2 is "Geographic and Executive Indexes"; and Volume 3 lists "New Associations and Projects."

lends clout to the Christian's quest for justice. It multiplies the individual's impact considerably. In terms of being a part of an activity which can and does make a significant difference in the public conduct of society, public pressure groups perhaps provide the most effective avenue of social action.

They also provide opportunity for evangelistic witness, bringing the Christian into contact with people in society whom one might not otherwise meet. Finally, such participation provides enriching social contacts, broadened experience and education, and a sense of spending oneself in meaningful pursuits.

ENGAGE

Group-Involvement Inventory

In the chart provided below, list all the voluntary groups of which you are a member or in which you participate. Briefly summarize the purpose of each group; then estimate how much time and money you invest in the group per month.

Group	Purpose	Time spent per month	Money contributed per month

Evaluating Your Group Involvements

Refer to the chart you filled out above.

1. How many of the groups to which you belong exist primarily "in themselves," for social relationships or the personal benefit of members?*

*You might classify a Bible study as existing for the personal benefit of the members, yet insofar as members apply God's Word in their lives and world, its effects can go far beyond that of a purely self-oriented group.

2. How many exist "for themselves," to work for their own interests in the larger community?

3. How many exist "for the public," to work for other groups or for the shared interest of the community as a whole?

4. Are there other groups in which you would like to participate but currently do not? Which group(s)? Why do you not participate currently?

5. If you face a time or energy shortage, are there groups in which you currently participate that you might consider leaving in order to participate in other groups which would help you better to fulfill your duty as a Christian? Which one(s)?

6. Are there groups in which you participate marginally but in which you would like to increase your involvement? Which one(s)?

7. Are there groups which you would like to investigate further before deciding whether or not to participate? Which one(s)?

Set up a time line for taking action on the decisions you stated above. For instance:

- By ___(date)___ I will begin/cease regularly participating in ___(group)___ .

- By ___(date)___ I will write for more information on ___(group)___ , and _____weeks after receiving the information, I will decide whether or not to participate.

Networking

Do you currently participate in a local group or groups that could profit from affiliating with a like-minded organization at the state or national level?

Do you currently participate in a state or national group or groups that could benefit from having an organization at the local level?

Why not take the initiative and explore the possibility of forming such ties? It could increase the group's effectiveness and thus multiply the impact of each member's involvement.

Choosing a Manageable Issue

Sharing Findings

Your three study groups should now present the findings from their research on the three top problem areas chosen by your group. Hand out the written reports of each group and allow the members sufficient time to skim each report. Then have a member of each group highlight its report and answer any questions. Entertain a brief time of discussion.

Prayer

Break up into several small groups for a time of prayer, seeking God's guidance upon the decision you face. Remember that prayer involves active listening for the still small voice of God as much as, or even more than, it involves our trying to communicate our thoughts and ideas to God.

Decision Making

Come back together as a group. Following the decision-making procedure that you voted to follow as part of your by-laws ("Engage," chapter 7, pages 83-84), choose the problem area on which your group desires to focus its efforts.

Purpose Statement

With your problem area and related research in mind, develop a statement of purpose. Refine your focus from the general problem area to one specific issue within that area. Your statement of purpose should state the intention of your group in regard to that issue. It may take the following form.

In light of *(here state the issue)*, it is the purpose of *(here state the name of your group)* to *(here state your purpose)*   .

For example, the purpose statement of the local nuclear armament study and action group might be as follows: In light of the growing threat to human life and welfare presented by the proliferation of nuclear armaments, it is the purpose of the Peace Council to follow in the steps of Christ as peacemakers in our community and world, opposing the buildup of nuclear weaponry, raising awareness in our community of the dangers of such a buildup, and affirming those acts and policies which make for peace.

Goals

Further refine your focus upon the issue by breaking down your purpose statement into goal statements. A goal should be both measureable and attainable; it should name a concrete act that can and will be performed by a certain date. It might take the following form.

By   *(when)*,   *(who)*   will   *(perform what)*
(if applicable, how many times)   .

List the goals that your group will work toward as a means of fulfilling its stated purpose. For example, some goals of the Peace Council might be the following:

As a means of opposing the buildup of nuclear weaponry,

- each member will serve for one month as legislative liaison, informing the membership about specific legislation coming before Congress for a vote;

- each member will contact his or her congressional representatives at least a week, if possible, before relevant legislation comes to a floor vote, expressing support or opposition to said legislation.

As a means of raising awareness in the community,

- by   *(date)*   the Peace Council will have organized and publicized a speakers bureau, making available resource persons from the Council who are willing to speak to local organizations and groups at no cost;

- once a year the Peace Council will produce a play, series of skits, or other public presentation, which dramatizes and educates people on nuclear armament issues.

Research

Continue your research, homing in on your specific issue area and seeking the information you will need to fulfill your goals most effectively. Keep your information organized in a notebook or file, so that group members will have access to it to add information or refer to the research already done.

10

Watchdogging Politics

In April a school district in a medium-size town asked teachers and other personnel if they would forego their pay raises as a means of avoiding lay-offs and helping the school out of financial difficulties. In July of the same year, the school superintendent wrote into the school budget an 8½ percent pay increase for himself and similar increases for other administrators. Several school board members, about to vote on the budget, were questioned about this pay increase. They admitted they had not been aware of it. They passed the budget anyway.

The Community Action Agency has been the most effective advocate and distributor of services for the low-income people in the industrial southern portion of a county. The agency now faces the possibility of going out of existence. Why? Human service funds have been transferred from the federal government to state governments for distribution. The states have the option of using the funds for purposes other than funding the Community Action Agencies, which would, in effect, abolish the agencies. The state administration, moreover, would like to see their demise as it has at times been a target of their advocacy efforts. The local newspapers carry no mention of this issue.

A small city has received a block of money from the federal government through revenue sharing. A major portion of the funds made available through revenue sharing has been taken from programs for the socially disadvantaged. Low-income people in this city not only lack sufficient income but also need better services in securing employment and legal aid. The infrastructure of the sections of the city in which they live is inadequate in terms of housing, transportation, safety, parks, and recreation. The city council decides, however, to spend the revenue-sharing money to provide sidewalks and a fire department in a newly developed section of the city. The voters are aware of the vote to spend the funds in this way but have no concept of the alternative choices for which the funds might have been spent.

None of these incidents made the newspapers. The majority of the citizens affected by these events never knew about them although they had to foot the bill for them.

In general, people know more about what goes on at the national level than they do about local politics. They know their national representatives better, and they have more familiarity with national issues. National representatives receive better media coverage and make a greater effort to communicate with constituents. In contrast, citizens tend to be ill-informed about who local officeholders are, what they do, and how they vote on specific issues.

Local newspapers often share a large portion of the blame for this situation. Although usually lacking enough solid local news to cover the front and back pages of their major news sections, they still do not have room (or, more probably, the energy) to provide close coverage of the city council or school board. Especially helpful would be coverage of how different officials voted on different issues, but rarely does such information make it into print.*

Despite the ideal behind a representative form of government—that all citizens have an equal opportunity to have their concerns represented by having an equal opportunity to hold office—the system doesn't function that way in reality. Ability, concern, and willingness to hold office are not enough. One needs wealth and/or connections in order to run successfully for public office. Hence we have a breakdown in the democratic processes; this results in a government that often is not representative of the citizenry. Even when officeholders do represent well, reflecting the views of those who elected them, they are subjected to few checks to determine if they actually are carrying out the people's interests. This information gap, particularly prevalent in local politics, can yield sorry results.

Since they have little to worry about in terms of accountability, it is no wonder that local officeholders often exhibit a lack of devotion and responsibility to their constituents. No wonder local politics are often afflicted with corruption.

*A newspaper that is reliable and sensitive to the needs of the community is a major contributor to an informed social consciousness. For practical guidelines on watchdogging your local paper, see *How to Appraise and Improve Your Daily Newspaper*, by David Bollier, (Washington, D.C.: Center for Study of Responsible Law, 1980).

Special interests too frequently dominate the scene. Friends of office-holders are awarded contracts, whether or not they give the best service at the best price. Business and industry seem to have a greater voice in local government than do residential taxpayers. Even the revenue-sharing programs of the federal government—to the extent that they have been serious and not a sham covering up reduced federal expenditures in vital areas—fail in many respects at the local level. Too often money has been taken from important and carefully defined federal programs and sent undesignated or with few guidelines to local bodies. Once there, it does not reach the poor and needy, who have little voice at the local level. Instead it is used for the special, pet interests of the community. The money appears at the local level as a bonus that can be spent for the extra fire engine or new sidewalks.

What can be done about this lack of government responsibility at the local level? How can local government be made more accountable to local citizens? How can citizens become more informed about what goes on in local government?

A group of citizens in Cambridge, Massachusetts, banded together to address these problems. The Cambridge Churchmen for Civic Responsibility (CCCR) agreed to cooperate as a group around a twofold purpose. They sought to be informed of the activities of the city council, the school board, and other agencies in order to have basic knowledge for intelligent political action; and they organized to act as a pressure group, expressing their views to local governing bodies.

Pastors, lay people, and church social action committees joined together to form the CCCR. They were drawn together by the common bond of being moved by their religious convictions to participate in the political process and to speak out on issues of social significance. Members felt free, nonetheless, to hold differing opinions on specific issues.

There were two types of membership in this organization. The regular membership contributed suggested dues of ten dollars per year. They received the *Bulletin,* the organization's medium of communication, and they had the privilege of having their views represented in the action phase of the CCCR's work. Social-action committees of churches were encouraged to participate as sustaining members, contributing dues of one hundred dollars per year.

Members were asked to give three hours every two weeks to cover and report upon the meetings of one specific agency or governmental group. These reports included the specific issues that came up in the meeting, how each officeholder voted on each issue, and what issues would be coming up in the future. The reports were printed in the *Bulletin*, which was published semi-monthly (see Illustration 1, on page 126). Members were also asked to work periodically on specific issues of special importance which might arise.

The members would thus keep informed about important issues in their community and would be prepared to make their voices heard when they felt it necessary. Not only did this keep the participants better informed as citizens, but it also made the local officeholders aware that they were being held accountable for how they used the power of their offices.

This accountability became especially apparent at election time. The voting records of the incumbents were on paper for anyone to examine. Challengers for the office were polled on specific issues. They were asked very specific questions in order to avoid the usual politically vague answers given by candidates. The results were published in the *Bulletin* (see Illustration 2, on pages 127-128), along with the voting recommendations of the director of the CCCR. His recommendations were based upon conclusions drawn from the voting reports and polling results prepared by CCCR members. Hence voter response to the work of the members throughout the year found direct expression at the voting booths. Given that the members of such a committee have contact with various other groups in the community, this flow of information to voters could have a significant impact in an election.

The CCCR also reported upon bills before the state legislature (see Illustration 3 on page 129). The conduct of state representatives is often as unknown as that of municipal officials. This is unfortunate because the state legislature has great power. The CCCR was selective in reporting on bills coming before the legislature, due to the preponderance of bills considered there.* They found it important, therefore, to know

---

*Several thousand bills may be submitted to a state legislature in one year. A group does not have the time to survey them all as they are found in the legislative bulletin; rather, one works through other groups. Advocacy and public pressure groups are knowledgeable about the key bills in their area of concern which have a chance to pass. For example, a group interested in legislation affecting children in Massachusetts would profit from talking with people at the state Office for Children. Another source of information would be a friendly legislator who might share his or her knowledge about prospective bills. Different legislators are usually recognized as knowledgeable about certain areas, such as welfare legislation or natural resources. Finally, the group could contact caucuses that have social goals with which they are comfortable. One such caucus would be the Democratic Study Group in Massachusetts. Contacting such a group would be helpful in receiving early information about pending legislation. It is important to be in touch with a network of groups pursuing goals about which your group is concerned. The critical information will emerge —if not in their literature, then through personal contacts.

what bills were up for consideration so as to act on the few that they considered important to their group. Crucial state legislature roll-call votes were recorded in the *Bulletin* (see Illustration 4 on page 130). The *Bulletin* also reported the voting record of their local U.S. Representative, Thomas P. O'Neill. Newspapers seldom report more than the major votes of Congress. Moreover, the representative's own literature usually presents only selected votes. Without seeing the overall record, voters can be misled as to their representative's performance on their behalf.

The fact that the CCCR involved people from many churches—clergy and laity alike—added to their clout. It gave them the political advantage of having a broad base of support. It also proved vital in the effort of information gathering, which was central to the CCCR's task. A strong church might be able to handle the task by itself, but it is best to include all who are interested and who can be benefited by it.

The CCCR director and founder, Robert Veatch, put in long, hard hours voluntarily. It might be advisable for a large organization to pay a part-time salary to a director. The CCCR director was assisted by field education students from Harvard Divinity School. The students, in turn, were under the supervision of a steering committee chosen by the members. They operated to inform and guide the members but were not essential to the conception of the organization. As is obvious from the description of the group's task, the volunteer work performed by members was indispensable. Members also gave clerical help in preparing the *Bulletin,* which they mimeographed for distribution.

In our society people can have effective political power if they are willing to organize for it. Too often groups seeking to prevent social change for justice or human need in a community are better organized than those who should be supporting the change. A watchdog organization, such as the CCCR, enables its members to act in favor of justice on *many* issues as they come up. The relatively small investment of time and support that such an organization requires yields great returns: a better informed, better empowered local citizenry and officeholders who are more responsive to those who elected them. It only takes twenty-five to one hundred people in a community giving an evening (three hours) every two weeks to community politics to change that community significantly. Christian citizens should order their priorities so as to be able to give that much time to community responsibilities.

To our knowledge, the Cambridge Churchmen for Civic Responsibility folded after its founder and director graduated from Harvard Graduate School and left the area. Such organizations often depend on the vision and energy of a single person and have difficulty being institutionalized. In later conversations the founder said that if he were to do it over again, he might try to get some foundational support for the activity. This would take some pressure off the organization's dependence upon merely voluntary motivation. But foundation money, even if procured, would only last until the enterprise was off the ground. Christian commitment should be sufficient to sustain such an effort.

In previous chapters we have considered how citizens might act in order to influence public policy. Watchdogging the performance of state and national leaders is as vital as watchdogging the local political scene. While you can rarely be present at sessions of the state and national legislatures, in contrast to city council and school board meetings, you can still participate in watchdogging through membership in a public pressure group organized to monitor state and national policymaking.

Digesting the information you receive from the public pressure group(s) to which you belong is only half of the watchdogging process. The other half lies in the cost of a postage stamp—your response to your state and national legislators letting them know how you feel about vital issues and about their voting record.

Network, a religious lobby for social justice, and Bread for the World have composed some helpful guidelines for contacting one's senators and representatives.[1] Many of the suggestions that follow (and others) can be found in their publications and those of similar organizations.

Letter writing can and does make a difference. Bread for the World, in urging people to contact their legislators concerning world hunger legislation, has quoted Illinois Representative Paul Simon: "Someone who sits down and writes a letter about hunger . . . almost literally has to be saving a life. . . ."[2]

The opinions that their constituents express play an important role in the decision making of legislators. They have been elected to Congress to represent those opinions. Congresspersons *do* read their mail, and many keep a record of how many constituents support or oppose certain bills.

In writing to one's legislators, remember that personal letters carry more clout than do form letters. Any information you can share, such as reprints of newspaper or magazine articles or data gained from research, may aid your congressperson by giving new insight; it also lends support to your position. Accounts of how the proposed legislation would affect you, your family, or your community add a great deal to the explanation of your position. Share well-thought-out opinions, not emotional appeals or prejudices.

Write about only one subject or legislative matter per letter. State the purpose of your letter in the first paragraph, and include the bill number and/or title of the legislation, if possible. Ask specific questions about the congressperson's stance on the legislation. This will ensure a response.

The best time to write is when the bill is in committee. That is when most of the work is done concerning the content of the bill and whether or not it will be recommended for a floor vote in the House or Senate. It helps to know, then, what committees your congresspersons are on. It is also valuable to write just before the bill comes before the House or Senate for a vote.

When the congressperson sends a reply, follow up with another letter in which you thank the person for his or her support or urge the person to reconsider his or her position. Explain your disapproval and/or send more information. You may also want to ask for more information if you feel you have received a vague response that avoids the issue. However, *do* send letters of commendation from time to time, particularly when your congressperson has taken a courageous stand on behalf of a position that you support.

To write to your U.S. representative, address your letter to:

The Honorable _____
The United States House of Representatives
Washington, D.C. 20515

To write to your U.S. senators, address your letter to:

The Honorable _____
The United States Senate
Washington, D.C. 20510

To telephone your congresspersons, dial the Capitol switchboard at 202-224-3121. Or you can call the home district office and leave a message; it will be relayed to Washington. Personal Opinion Message telegrams and Mailgrams are a bit more expensive but are speedy options for communicating and have the advantage of putting your message in writing.

A visit to one's senator or representative is a very effective way of influencing that person on a concern which is important to you. Perhaps the best opportunity to visit a respresentative is when he or she is visiting the home district. On a home visit the representative feels he or she is meeting a more representative cross section of voters than those who visit the Washington office.

To make an appointment, call the representative's district office. In your request, state your topic of concern and who will be coming. A day or so before the appointment, confirm the time by phone. If the congressperson is not available, ask to meet with a legislative aide.

As you prepare for the visit, find out the congressperson's voting record and position on your topic of concern. Acquaint yourself with background information on the topic and know what legislation has been proposed relating to it. If you are going as a group, decide who will initiate the discussion and who will make what key points. Be positive and constructive. Don't criticize the congressperson but remain firm and clear in explaining your position. Don't let the congressperson dominate the discussion. Make specific requests, ask for commitments, and leave a short written summary of your position. Follow up with a thank-you note and maintain contact by mail.

Public officials are not the only ones to whom we should write letters as a form of effective social action. Editors of newspapers, managers of television stations, and corporate magnates also should be included in our correspondence. Many of the characteristics of letters to congresspersons should apply to these letters as well.

Brevity is even more important in a letter to an editor. Editors usually limit published letters to 250 to 300 words and generally require that you include your name, address, and telephone number. The tone of these letters should be positive—even in a letter of criticism. Sarcasm, self-righteousness, or emotional excesses do not accomplish what should be the goals of such a letter: correcting facts, sharing a differing opinion, or suggesting a different outlook.

To give feedback on television commercials, you can write to the following organization (send a copy of your letter to the president of the company that manufactures the product): Action Line, Direct Mail Marketing Association, 6 East 43rd St., New York, NY 10017. To give feedback on television programming, you can write directly to the networks:

—Audience Information, ABC-TV, 1330 Ave. of the Americas, New York, NY 10019

—Audience Services, CBS Television Network, 51 W. 52nd St., New York, NY 10019

—Audience Services, NBC-TV, 30 Rockefeller Plaza, New York, NY 10020

If you are writing to an advertiser or manufacturer, you can look for the company's address in *Standard and Poor's Register of Corporations, Directors and Executives.* To find to what conglomerate a product belongs, try the *Trade Names Directory.* Another helpful volume for these concerns is the *Standard Directory of Advertisers.* The *Govern-*

ment Organizational Manual will help you find your target in the federal bureaucracy. Your public librarian can help you to locate these reference works.

You have an opportunity to get your concerns onto the airwaves when a station presents in an unbalanced way a view which you oppose. Under the "Fairness Doctrine" you are entitled to equal time to make a rebuttal and present your views. Various organizations have prepared helpful guidelines for making use of equal-time opportunities.[3]

These simple kinds of involvements don't take a huge amount of time. Yet they can be effective and vital means of watchdogging politics at the local, state, and national levels. Responsible citizens who care can make a big difference in how responsive and responsible government, business, and the media are to the people.

ENGAGE

Civic Responsibility Quiz

Fill in the following blanks with the appropriate responses.

1. The names of the U.S. senators from my state are _____

   and _____.

2. The name of my U.S. representative is _____.

3. The name of my state senator is _____.

4. The name of my state representative is _____.

5. The name of the mayor/city manager of my town is _____.

6. The name of the city council member who represents the area

   in which I live is _____.

7. The names of at least three local school board members are

   _____, _____, _____.

Fill in the following blanks (8, 9, 10) with the response that best describes your involvement. Choose from the following responses:

   all

   most

   some

   few

   no

8. I vote in _____ presidential elections and am familiar with _____ names on the ballot.

9. I vote in _____ statewide elections/referenda and am familiar with _____ names/issues on the ballot.

10. I vote in _____ local elections/referenda and am familiar with _____ names/issues on the ballot.

Fill in the following blanks with the appropriate responses.

11. In the past year, I have attended _____ city council meetings.

12. In the past year, I have attended _____ local school board meetings.

13. In the past year, I have attended meetings of other local governing bodies _____ times.

14. In the past year, I have contacted my state legislators _____ times.

15. In the past year, I have contacted my U.S. representative and/or my U.S. senators _____ times.

Now take a few minutes to look over your answers to this quiz; then complete the following sentence by circling the appropriate response:

The adjective(s) which best describes my civic involvement is(are)

committed	apathetic
indifferent	interested
enthusiastic	ignorant
so-so	attempting
dominating	retreating
growing	selective
minimal	constant
pessimistic	hopeful

You may wish to share the adjective(s) you chose to describe yourself with your other group members and explain why you chose it (them).

Not Just Wagging Our Tails

Does a watchdogging organization such as the one described in this chapter sound like something that could benefit your community? Why or why not? In what way?

Considering the size and complexity of your community, how many volunteer workers would be necessary to cover the meetings of local government bodies and to publish the newsletter: 10? 25? 100? What persons and groups in your community might be interested in committing themselves to such a venture? Beyond the volunteer workers, are there people who might support the endeavor by subscribing to the newsletter?

Today your group will be considering strategies for fulfilling the goals and general purpose that you set down at your last meeting. Perhaps watchdogging, on some scale, will enter into the strategy you develop. Or perhaps, if your group has been unable to settle on any one issue but wishes to serve your community, you might consider initiating and developing a watchdogging organization in your community as your group activity.

Research Results

Look at the results of your research to date. Does it confirm that the issue you have chosen seems manageable for your group to address?

Look at your group. Do you seem to have a spirit of unity as you progress in addressing this issue? Is your overwhelming spirit one of optimism, pessimism, indifference, or confidence?

Indifference is fatal. If your group is largely indifferent toward addressing this issue, you had better reassess your goals. Choose a different issue or commit yourselves to rooting out the indifference and seeking renewed enthusiasm. Or if your members are motivated to become involved in socially caring ministry but just can't come to a consensus, perhaps you should function as a support group as members involve themselves in the various ministries to which they feel called.

If the term "pessimistic" describes your group, perhaps you have chosen an issue which is more than you can handle. Consider addressing a more manageable issue within the larger issue, or joining forces with a more experienced group that might have better resources for addressing this issue.

If your group is optimistic or confident, good! You probably have chosen a manageable issue and set realistic goals. Don't be falsely optimistic or overconfident. Continue at a careful pace, seeking God's guidance and blessing at every juncture.

Finally, a note about research. The research you do and the results you derive from it should guide you as you move to address actively the issue you have chosen. Your research should give you a sense of the background and extent of your issue. It should help you find resources for addressing the issue; it should make you aware of possible pitfalls or obstacles; and it should guide you in choosing your strategy.

Beware, however, of "paralysis by analysis." Don't make the research stage an end in itself, so that you never move to action. Research is comfortable, for it involves little risk of failure. In the long run, though, you accomplish little unless you act upon what you know.

You should continue to learn, investigate, and grow even as you progress into the action phase of your involvement. But don't mistake knowing for doing.

Defining Your Strategy

Look at the goals you have chosen to achieve. Defining your strategy involves answering this question: What kind(s) of action will be necessary to achieve these goals? Your answer may be one or several of the following types of action:

watchdogging	picketing ·	letter-writing
lobbying	teaching	consciousness-raising
transporting	investigating	going door-to-door
interviewing	fund-raising	administering
helping	donating	suing
rehabilitating	organizing	boycotting
acting	informing	preaching
counseling	cooking	listening

Whatever your goals may be, reaching them will surely involve the following types of action:

Loving God and loving every neighbor;
Praying for guidance, wisdom, and strength;
Receiving the help and the presence of the Holy Spirit;
Giving of yourself;
Obeying our Lord Jesus Christ;
Being a new creature.

Break your goals down into the steps that will be necessary to achieve them. Each step may entail a different type of action. Decide what action will be necessary for each step.

Once you have determined the necessary steps and the action entailed in each step, you are ready to define your overall strategy. Organize these steps in the most feasible sequence for your group to perform. To simplify this procedure, you may want to write each step on a single three-by-five-inch card. Also note on the card the number of the goal to which that step corresponds. Arrange the cards on a table in a sequence that moves you progressively toward meeting your goals. Decide whether you can, should, and/or desire to address more than one goal at once.

Some steps involve laying foundations for action; obviously your group will have to perform these first. Some steps assume that other action steps have already been completed; for instance, you wouldn't announce a boycott without first contacting the offending company, explaining your grievance, and asking for voluntary cooperation. Take such strategizing into consideration as you plan your action.

Once you have completed this task, you may wish to affix the cards to a bulletin board or wall for further scrutiny, possible change, and future reference as you move into the action phase.

The next step, which your group should accomplish at your next meeting, involves deciding upon a timeline—when should each step be begun and completed? It also involves deciding upon a division of labor—who will perform each step? Before moving on to this step, make sure that the group is satisfied with the strategy that you have set up together. Are there any gaps? Any overlaps? Can you achieve each step on your own? If not, where can you get some support?

<u>Illustration 1</u>

CCCR BULLETIN   JANUARY 15, 1970   PAGE 2

1969 CITY COUNCIL ROLL CALLS

The CCCR Bulletin presents below a summary of the City Council votes for October through December of 1969. For earlier 1969 votes see volume one, number one. Note that beginning with this issue we are presenting the actual "yes" and "no" votes of the Councillors abandoning the plus and minus system of the previous report.

	ACKERMANN	CRANE	DANEHEY	GOLDBERG	HAYES	MAHONEY	VELLUCCI	WHEELER	MAYOR SULLIVAN
Y = Yes, N = No, P = Present, A = Absent									
20. RENT CONTROL. Motion to seek advisory opinion on rent control from Cambridge voters. Vellucci amendment to exempt all 2-, 3-, and 4-family, owner-occupied units. 10/6/69	N	P	P	P	Y	P	Y	N	Y
21. RENT CONTROL. Motion to seek advisory opinion on rent control from Cambridge voters. 10/6/69	Y	N	N	N	N	Y	P	Y	N
22. STATIONERY APPROPRIATION. Motion by Councillor Hayes to *reconsider* appropriation of $167.25 for stationery for a councillor, in order to refer to the finance committee to examine the high cost of the stationery. 10/28/69	Y	N	Y	Y	Y	Y	N	Y	A
23. CRA APPOINTMENTS. Vellucci motion to *table* consideration of the appointments of John A. Lunn and Robert W. Bright to the Cambridge Redevelopment Authority. (Lunn is a member of the MIT Corporation; Bright, a past president of the National Alliance of Post Office Employees and a resident of the redevelopment area. Amidst demands that both CRA appointments be low-income, development area residents.) 11/10/69	Y	Y	Y	Y	N	Y	Y	N	Y

Illustration 2

These questions were asked of candidates for city council.* Answers of the various candidates follow.

Questions

1. On March 24, 1969, the council voted against a motion putting the council on record in favor of the appointment of one Black and one renewal area resident to the Cambridge Redevelopment Authority. How would you have voted?

2. On June 30, 1969, the council voted against the rent control proposal submitted by the Cambridge Housing Convention. How would you have voted?**

3. On August 7, 1969, the council voted against the rent control proposal submitted as an initiative petition by the Cambridge Rent Control Referendum Campaign. How would you have voted?***

4. On September 8, 1969, the council voted to rescind the driveway cutting permit for the Jack-in-the-Box Restaurant to be located at Prospect and Cambridge Streets. The restaurant was opposed by certain area residents and the local Model Cities Agency. How would you have voted on the motion to rescind?

CCCR BULLETIN   NOVEMBER 1, 1969   PAGE 3

COUNCIL CANDIDATES POLL

NAME	QUESTION			
	1	2	3	4
Byrle Breny 1039 Massachusetts Avenue 354-4812	yes	yes	yes	yes
James W. Caragianes Hdq: 265 Pearl St. 868-9853	yes	yes	no	yes
L. David Cleveland 261 Broadway	yes	no	no	"open"
Daniel J. Clinton 12 Speridakis Terrace	yes			
Thomas Coates (CCA) Hdq: 201 Western Ave. 491-9666	yes	yes	yes	yes

*A similar poll was taken for the school committee election.
**This question is too weak because a person could have significantly different motivations for voting no. The proposal was quite moderate.
***This proposal was more thorough.

Daniel F. Connelly 14 Chalk St.	yes	yes	yes	yes
Robert P. Moncreiff (CCA) Hdq: 11 Gray Gardens East 876-4009	no	no	no	yes
E. Peter Mullane 45 Tremont St.	yes	yes	yes	yes
Steven R. Nelson 944 Massachusetts Ave.	yes	yes	yes	yes
Henry F. Owens III 3 Yerxa Road	yes	no	no	yes
Raymond L. Proulx 4 Day St.	yes	yes	yes	yes
Leonard J. Russell 5 Hawthorne Pk., 864-8777	yes	yes	yes	yes
Jeremiah V. Shea 114 Elm St., TR6-1312	yes	yes	yes	yes
Gustave M. Solomons (CCA) 85 Inman St.	yes	yes	no	yes
Sarah J. Ullman (Socialist Workers) 118 Kinnaird St.	yes	no	yes	present

Illustration 3

CCCR BULLETIN   FEBRUARY 15, 1970

STATE BILLS FOR 1970

A large number of bills have been filed for the 1970 session of the General Court of Massachusetts which are of interest to churchmen and other citizens. The list below which contains many of them is based in part on the work of the Legislative Committee of the Massachusetts Council of Churches. The CCCR Bulletin elsewhere in this issue and in future issues will describe in more detail some of these bills. The name of the legislative committee handling the bill is also given.

HOUSING

S–47, S 76, S 239 Increasing state's annual contributions for housing the elderly. — Urban Affairs

S–240, S 1198, S 1162, H 579 Increasing state's provisions for housing of low-income persons.

S–518 Housing court for Boston. — Judiciary

S–529 Compensating tenants forced to relocate because of eminent domain proceedings. — Judiciary

S–531 Reimbursing persons displaced by eminent domain proceedings for portions of increased interest paid in purchase of new dwelling. — Judiciary

S–587, H 1058, H 1956, H 2378, H 3108, H 4256 Authorizing local rent control. — Local Affairs

H–2710 Authorizing rent control for Cambridge and Brookline. — Local Affairs

H–1747 Authorizing rent control for Cambridge. — Local Affairs

H–363, H 1175 Extending provisions of rental assistance program. — Urban Affairs

H–580 Authorizing rehabilitation of housing in depressed areas. — Urban Affairs

H–2069 Amending zoning enabling act to make special provisions for low- and moderate-income housing. — Urban Affairs

H–2330 Facilitating receipt of federal assistance toward home ownership by certain lower-income persons. — Federal Financial Assist.

H–2903 Insuring proper relocation housing. — Judiciary

H–4364 Alleviating housing needs and costs through provision of reasonable construction standards. — Urban Affairs

H–4749 Establishing uniform state building code and agencies for administering it. — State Administ.

Illustration 4

1969 STATE HOUSE VOTES

	KEY			F	H	L	N	T
				L	I	O	E	O
	Y = YEA			A	C	M	W	O
	N = NAY			H	K	B	M	M
	A = ABSENT			E	E	A	A	E
				R	Y	R	N	Y
				T		D		
				Y		I		

1. GENERIC DRUGS. H5006 to include generic names with brand names on prescriptions. A motion to send the bill to the Supreme Judical Court failed, 160-65. 4/22/69
   N N N Y N

2. MCAD. Motion to *kill* a bill to extend coverage of anti-discrimination laws to all 2-family houses. Motion to kill passed 130-85. 4/30/69
   A Y Y N Y

3. PUNISHING DISRUPTIONS AT UNIVERSI-TIES. Motion to suspend rules and consider punitive measures against disruption of programs at state universities. Failed 143-76 (2/3 required) 5/12/69
   N Y Y N A

4. REDUCING SIZE OF HOUSE. Motion to send the question of cutting the House to a special committee, *postponing a vote* for this year. Passed in Joint Session 164-105. 5/14/69
   Y Y Y N Y

5. METCO FUNDING. Amendment of the Speaker to increase the appropriation for Metco. Passed 150-56. 5/19/69
   Y Y N Y N

6. AID TO PRIVATE SCHOOLS. A first step in a constitutional amendment to allow public funding of teachers' salaries in private and parochial schools. Passed 190-75. 6/18/69
   Y Y Y N Y

7. TAXES. Motion increasing revenue through income tax reform. Passed 121-110. 7/15/69
   Y Y N Y N

8. AUTO INSURANCE. Motion substituting the "basic protection" plan for a Senate study. Failed 100-135. 7/29/69
   Y Y Y Y N

9. PRESIDENTIAL PRIMARY. Motion which would have substituted a resolve for the bill to require the names of all presidential candidates to appear on the ballot. Failed 108-11. 7/30/69
   N A Y N Y

Illustration 5

CCCR BULLETIN   May 25, 1970   page 4

1970 O'NEILL VOTES

1. HR 15149	Foreign Aid Appropriation. Jan. 27, 1970	Paired for
2. HR 13111	Appropriation for Departments of Labor and Health, Education, and Welfare. Attempt to override presidential veto. January 27, 1970	Yes
3. HR 14864	Defense Facilities and Industrial Security Act authorizing measures to protect defense production and classified information released to defense industry against subversion. January 29, 1970	No
4. HR 15165	Creation of a Population Commission. Feb. 18, 1970	Yes
5. HR 15931	Labor-HEW Appropriation. *Motion to recommit* with instructions to report it with authority for President to withhold 2½% of the funds. Feb. 19, 1970	No
6. HR 15931	Labor-HEW Appropriation. Feb. 19, 1970	Yes
7. S 2823	Mental Health Centers. Adoption of a conference report to extend for three years the Community Mental Health Centers Construction Act. Feb. 26, 1970	Yes
8. HR 15728	Naval Vessel Loans. Passage of a bill authorizing loans of 11 surplus Navy ships and submarines to foreign countries. March 23, 1970	Yes
9. HR 15628	Foreign Military Sales Act. Passage of a bill extending the program and authorizing appropriations. March 24, 1970	Yes
10. H Res 844	Internal Security Committee Appropriation of $450,000. March 25, 1970	Yes
11. HR 4148	Water Quality Improvement Act of 1970. March 25, 1970	Yes
12. HR 514	Elementary and Secondary Education Act Amendments. Aid to federally impacted areas and other education legislation. April 7, 1970	Yes

11

Seeking Justice Through Noncooperation

The two men had been warned by the authorities never again to preach in Jesus' name. Although they were otherwise law-abiding citizens, the next day they were right back on the streets, preaching to the crowds that gathered around them. They were arrested, beaten, and thrown into jail.

He refused to register for the draft. It went against his conscience, he said, for he strongly sensed God guiding him to refrain from military involvement. The judge sentenced him to 250 hours of community service and told him to register for the draft within thirty days or face a fine and imprisonment. When questioned by reporters after the trial, he said he did not plan to register.

During the busy shopping week before Christmas of 1969, the black community of a small Mississippi town began a boycott of all the white businesses in town. The boycott came as an immediate response to the unprovoked mass arrest of local religious and civil rights leaders, as well as a group of young black children. The black community used the boycott to pressure the all-white political and law-enforcement system to drop their phony charges and free the prisoners. So successful was the boycott that the black community enlarged their list of demands to include fair hiring practices, the paving of streets in the black sector of town, and desegregation of all public facilities, including the schools.

During the years in which America allowed slavery, many people opened their homes and churches to runaway slaves and gave the slaves help as they trekked toward freedom. This movement grew into an organized network known as the Underground Railroad. Many of those involved were law-abiding citizens and active church members. Nevertheless, in persisting to help the slaves, they were breaking a law of the land. The slaves, if caught, had to be returned to their masters, and those helping them faced prosecution.

In the late 1970s a group calling themselves the Clamshell Alliance staged a mass sit-in on the grounds of the proposed nuclear power plant at Seabrook, New Hampshire. The group included both adults and children. Organized in opposition to the construction of the plant, they staged the sit-in as an attempt to prevent construction materials from being brought onto the site. Police were called in to move the people to make way for the trucks. Although the sit-in was a nonviolent one, many participants were arrested.

These are examples of a path to justice known as strategic noncoop- eration.* In each case those involved were acting in response to a law, a requirement, or a situation which they felt to be unjust or unconstitutional. Due to their perception of injustice in the existing legal system, they felt constrained to disobey or disregard the law in order to promote true justice.

In some cases, such as that of the draft resister, noncooperation comes more as a response of personal conscience than as a strategy for social change. It can, nevertheless, result in social change because it draws public attention to a law or a situation which the public also feels to be unjust but which previously has gone unnoticed or unquestioned.

In other cases, such as that of the Underground Railroad or of underground churches in communist countries, the noncooperation must be secret. In such cases it is not so much a strategy for social change as it is a means of clandestinely promoting justice within an unjust system. Nonetheless, change is brought about when those with an impetus for freedom find ways to act in accord with that impetus. On the one hand, slaves escaped to freedom; on the other hand, believers freed their spirits in unfettered worship.

What makes strategic noncooperation an effective method of social change? It is based upon the fact that, in order for social organizations to function properly, the members must consent and submit to the rules and leaders of the organization, whether it is a nation, a club, a business, or an economic system. Since the members voluntarily grant power to those in authority, they can also voluntarily withhold that power. If

*It is also known as nonviolent direct action.

those who customarily cooperate refuse to do so, they can cause even an institution with immense power to falter. Their noncooperation draws public attention to the injustice which they are protesting, and the offending organization finds itself in an awkward position. The cloak of presumed goodness has been whisked away, and the institution's actual practices are thrown open to public scrutiny.

Part of the power of the strategy of noncooperation lies in making the existing situation so uncomfortable or costly for the offending institution that it will voluntarily change in order to return to normalcy— minus the offensive practice or law. Important factors in this process are the loss of prestige for the institution, the nuisance of dealing with the resisters, the difficulty of carrying out normal functions, and the internal division that occurs as the protest movement picks up followers within the institution's own ranks. The institution's desire to do what is just is prodded by its economic self-interest. The organization can no longer calculate profits or carry on normal business as it has in the past; important concepts of right and of justice are now being forced into the picture by those protesting the institution's practices.

The success of the protest depends upon the breadth of public outrage, how effectively it is channeled into a form of noncooperation that can weaken and demoralize the offending institution, and the relative strength of the institution to stand or fall in the face of the noncooperation. For instance, "the United Farm Workers estimate that a consumer boycott needs the participation of only 2 to 3 percent of the population to succeed, and 10 percent participation would critically affect a producer within a few days."[1]

Strategic noncooperation can take many forms. It may involve only the breaking of a norm or disruption of an expected pattern, as when Solidarity supporters under martial law in Poland sang the national anthem and substituted their own lyrics. Other more aggressive forms of noncooperation include sit-ins, strikes, boycotts, picketing, and civil disobedience. In *none* of these forms, however, should violence be employed.

Use of violence in a noncooperation effort only weakens the possibility for success. Those involved in noncooperation must not only draw attention to the injustice they oppose, but in order to have credibility in the eyes of the public, they must also show forth a moral position superior to that of the offending institution. Use of violence or the destruction of property will in all probability make a hypocrisy of their superior moral position.

Can Christians avail themselves of this strategy for social change?

Does strategic noncooperation conflict with the biblical perspective on how Christians should conduct themselves in society?

Three statements in Scripture succinctly summarize how Christians should relate to the institutions of their society. 1 Peter 2:13 commands, "Submit yourselves for the Lord's sake to every [human ordinance]. . . ." Romans 12:2 begins, "Do not conform any longer to the pattern of this world . . ." and Amos 5:15 (RSV) calls us to "establish justice in the gate!"

We can immediately see a tension among these three mandates. Is the command to submit to every human ordinance an absolute one? That is, does our obligation to obey the law mean that we should never disobey the law? What if the law calls us to do something that conflicts with a command of God? What if a law impedes our worship or our witness in word and deed? How can we always submit to human authority and still obey the commands not to conform to this world's pattern and to establish justice in the gate?

We can immediately see a tension among these three mandates. Is the command to submit to every human ordinance an absolute one? That is, does our obligation to obey the law mean that we should never disobey the law? What if the law calls us to do something that conflicts with a command of God? What if a law impedes our worship or our witness in word and deed? How can we always submit to human authority and still obey the commands not to conform to this world's pattern and to establish justice in the gate?

Romans 13 and 1 Peter 2:13-17, two classic New Testament passages calling for Christians to submit to earthly authority, shed some light on this tension. Both passages deal with an issue of church discipline: the temptation to misuse Christian freedom. In some of the early churches, a number of believers got so caught up in their newfound freedom in Christ that they assumed they could also live free from familial and social obligations. Thus, the apostles found some believers sloughing off the responsibilities of being faithful in marriage, of living according to moral standards, of performing their jobs, or of obeying their masters if they were slaves,[2] and also of obeying the authority of secular government. These writings of the apostles, then, came as correctives to this abuse of Christian freedom. They affirmed that the Christians needed to maintain their social responsibilities, which included submitting to human authorities. Government was instituted by God to perform the good functions of maintaining order, establishing justice, and punishing wrong-doers. What an affront to the body of Christ if believers should have to be punished for shirking public responsibility in the name of Christian freedom! As Peter wrote, "Live as free [people], but do not use your freedom as a cover-up for evil; live as servants of God" (1 Peter 2:16).

In context, therefore, these passages cannot be interpreted as commanding the Christian never to disobey human authority. In addition, such an interpretation neglects the witness of other passages of Scripture, as well as the limits drawn within these passages. Both passages point to government as established by God, hence coming under God's authority. When government fulfills the functions that God established it to perform, obedience to government follows as a necessary part of our service to the Lord. However, when government attempts to assert *its* authority over God's, neglecting or perverting the functions for which it was established, Christian obedience to such government could amount to sacrilege.

The limits upon human subordination to government implied in these passages and in Jesus' words in Matthew 22:21, "Give to Caesar what is Caesar's, *and to God what is God's*," came as a novel idea in that day. The norm was for political and religious claims to be tied together in one system; religion, politics, social relations, and economics were so intertwined that there was little chance for any independent religious criticism of the practices. These Christian teachings debunked such a regard for government, allowing for criticism of government when it violated God's purposes.

Scripture provides many examples of believers who found it necessary to disobey human law in order to obey God. Daniel, Shadrach, Meshack, and Abednego refused to participate in emperor worship and continued to worship the living God. In so doing, they directly violated Babylonian law and were sent to torturous deaths. God intervened, however, and saved their lives. God blessed their obedience to the one true God, in defiance of human authority that tried to usurp God's divinity.

In seeking the release of the captive Israelites, Moses tried first to work through the existing legal system. However, the pharaoh consistently refused to do justice, ultimately withdrawing his permission for the Israelites to leave after they had already begun their exodus upon his bidding. While still in his jurisdiction, they nonetheless defiantly disobeyed his edict for their return. They continued to march out boldly (Exodus 14:8). They experienced God's deliverance as God opened the Red Sea for their passage but closed the sea over Pharaoh and his armies.

Even before the Exodus, the Hebrew midwives had to decide between obeying the pharaoh and obeying God. They chose to violate Pharaoh's command by sparing the newborn sons of the Hebrew women. God honored them for their disobedience of the king's edict (Exodus 1:15-21).

In the New Testament, we see other examples of believers disobeying government authority in order to be true to God. The Sanhedrin, Jewish leaders who had been endowed with authority by the Roman government, arrested the apostles and threw them in jail, ordering them to stop teaching in Jesus' name. During the night, the angel of the Lord delivered the apostles and directed them to return to the temple courts and preach the Good News. The apostles were again called before the Sanhedrin. "We gave you strict orders not to teach in his name," said the high priest. "Yet you have filled Jerusalem with your teaching and are determined to make us guilty of this man's blood." The reply of Peter and the apostles? "We must obey God rather than [humans]!" (Acts 5:28-29).

Not every situation seems so clear-cut. As we seek to glorify God through obedience to God's commands to submit to human authority, not to conform to this world's pattern, and to establish justice in the gate, we sometimes find ourselves facing conflicting claims and duties. At times we must make some very difficult ethical decisions.

In making such decisions, it can be helpful to distinguish among the types of duty we owe. Duties arise out of the relationships that we have with God, with other people, and with ourselves. Our relationship with God as our Creator and Redeemer results in our duty to love God, honor God, and obey God. The duty that we owe to God could be called a primary duty; no other type of duty can assume greater priority in our lives.

We owe primary duties to other people, also. The fulfilling of a promise is a primary duty. Protecting the life of another person is a primary duty, as is seeking the well-being of others by ensuring that their basic needs are met.

We also have secondary duties. These involve fulfilling the claims of custom, etiquette, efficiency, or utility. For instance, arriving at functions on time is a secondary duty. Waiting patiently in line and mowing the lawn are others. A secondary duty can never have a higher claim upon us than a primary duty. That is, we cannot fail to perform a primary duty in order to perform a secondary duty. For example, we cannot pass by an accident victim needing help because we are rushing to arrive at a meeting on time. In this case our actual duty—the right decision in a given situation—must be the primary duty to help the victim.

At times, a secondary duty becomes a primary duty because we *promise* to perform it. Suppose you have a reputation for being late, and you have promised your boss you will arrive at an important meeting on time. If you arrive late, you chance losing your job. You leave for the meeting in plenty of time, but on your way you happen upon an accident. You are the first to arrive on the scene, and you see that people are injured. Now, in determining your actual duty, you face a conflict among at least three primary duties: your duty to help the injured, your duty to keep your promise, and your duty to earn a living for your family. When faced with such a decision, one must prioritize among the primary duties according to which one(s) most directly affect basic human rights, including the right to life and to having basic needs met.

The right decision—the actual duty—in this case would be to help the injured. Yet if you made the right decision and stopped to help, why do you feel so badly about breaking your promise to your boss— even if your boss didn't fire you? Because an unfulfilled primary duty still exerts a claim upon us, even though we couldn't fulfill it because we had to choose a greater duty as our actual duty. Our sense of regret or shame flows from this unmet claim.

God's Word, the counsel of the Holy Spirit, and God's grace help us in our decision making. We act upon what we know of God's will as recorded in Scripture; we seek guidance and strength from the Holy Spirit; and we know the assurance of God's grace as we face the results of our decisions.

Every decision we make has what could be called right-making characteristics and wrong-making characteristics. Right-making characteristics are the primary claims that we are able to meet by making that decision. Wrong-making characteristics are the primary claims that go unmet as a result of making that decision. Hence in our example, fulfilling the primary duty to save human life was a right-making characteristic. Breaking the promise and risking loss of one's job were wrong-making characteristics. Yet the saving of life greatly outweighed the wrong-making characteristics. In making tough ethical decisions, the quality of the claims upon us matters more than the quantity of claims upon us.

These kinds of considerations are important when we consider whether or not to participate in strategic noncooperation. Does the good we seek exert a greater claim upon us than the law or custom we must break in order to seek that good? Consider the following situation.

In the year 1829, the state of Georgia enacted a law requiring the

Cherokees to give up their claim to ownership of their land in that state. As a restraint upon the missionaries who would stand up for the rights of the Cherokees, the law further ordered missionaries either to acknowledge the law and obtain a license to preach or to leave the state.

The Reverend Samuel A. Worcester and Dr. Elizur Butler faced an extremely difficult decision among primary duties: the duty to obey the law, the duty to fulfill their calling to minister among the Cherokees, their duty to maintain a clear conscience before God, and their duty to uphold the rights of the Cherokees to ownership of their land—their means of existence.

The two missionaries chose to defy the law; they would not publicly acknowledge it, and they would not leave their work among the Cherokees. For this they went to jail.

How did they arrive at the decision? They argued that the Cherokees needed the support of the missionaries in their efforts to retain their rights. Worcester and Butler felt that the primary duty of upholding the cause of justice for the oppressed had more right-making characteristics than abiding by a law which they knew to be unjust, even though the decision resulted in their being jailed. As Worcester put it, he was not acting from political expediency but from "clear moral obligation—a question of right or wrong—of keeping or violating the commands of God. . . ."[3]

Their obligation to obey the government nonetheless continued as an unmet claim upon the missionaries; hence it was a wrong-making characteristic of their decision. At the same time, their act of civil disobedience showed a *respect* for law and order: they publicly disobeyed this law because they felt that it did not meet the high standards of justice which laws are intended to uphold. They felt that the law was not only unfair and unconstitutional but was in conflict with God's claims upon them. They further showed respect for law and order by making their actions open to the public and the state and by being willing to accept the consequences of their action under law, in other words, being jailed.

Civil disobedience and other forms of strategic noncooperation are not alternatives to seeking justice through political involvement. Rather, before engaging in such protest one should exhaust every other possible resolution to the situation through legal or established means. Political involvement is necessary to complete the strides made toward justice through strategic noncooperation, for it is through the political process that unjust laws are replaced by just ones.

Can Christians participate in strategic noncooperation as a means toward social change? That is a question which in a general sense can be answered, "Yes." Yet in each specific case, the Christian must weigh before God and one's conscience the right-making and wrong-making characteristics of participating or failing to do so.

ENGAGE

Minicases

Following are two minicases in which the characters face decisions. Using the method described in this chapter, try to discern the primary duties, the secondary duties, and the actual duty of the character(s) in each case. Then list the right-making characteristics and the wrong-making characteristics of each decision. Use the chart provided on page 142 for noting your answers.

Minicase 1: Mary Rose, the widowed mother of four young children, belongs to the tenant association in her inner-city apartment building. The absentee landlord has let the place get very run-down; the roof leaks and necessary repairs to plumbing and appliances have gone undone. The tenant association is planning a rent strike until the landlord makes the repairs. He has said that he will evict immediately anyone who does not pay the rent. This has frightened many of the tenants, including Mary Rose. Yet the potential success of the rent strike depends upon a high percentage of tenant participation.

Examine the elements of Mary Rose's decision.

Minicase 2: The social-action committee of ABC church plans to encourage the congregation to support a United Farm Worker's boycott of a local supermarket chain which carries nonunion produce. A manager in one of the stores is a member of ABC church and has been a Christian for only a year. She calls the chairperson of the social-action committee and asks them not to support the boycott because her store can't afford to lose the business.

Examine the elements of the social-action committee's decision.

Developing a Timeline and Division of Labor

You may want to perform this step as a whole group, or you may want to assign it to a task force made up, for instance, of a representative from each committee.

By now you have determined your strategy, including the sequence of each step to be performed. Developing a timeline involves assigning a date by which each step should be completed. Keep in mind the time commitments of your group members and the length of time your group

MINICASE 1

Primary Duties	Secondary Duties	Actual Duty

Right-making Characteristics	Wrong-making Characteristics

MINICASE 2

Primary Duties	Secondary Duties	Actual Duty

Right-making Characteristics	Wrong-making Characteristics

as a whole has agreed to stay together to address your chosen issue. Try to be realistic about how long each step will take, from beginning to completion. You will, of course, have some overlap among steps, but if certain steps cannot be started until another step has been completed, make sure your timeline reflects that sequence. Write the beginning date and completion date for each step in red on the appropriate card. In blue or green, note on each card approximately how many people from which committee(s) will be needed to complete that step.

Committees should then meet to divide and organize their labor for completing those tasks for which they are responsible. The group as a whole should also come together so that any questions or problems can be raised and so that the group can finalize details for steps in which the group as a whole must act together. You may find some new and exciting ideas coming up in these sessions, which might improve your strategy. Be open to them.

Move to Action

Begin to carry out your strategy as planned, step by step. If problems arise (such as members not carrying out their tasks), refer back to the organizational decisions you made about accountability and group discipline.

Prior to taking certain steps that may create anxiety for the group, it could prove helpful to ponder the following questions: If everything goes wrong in this step, what are the worst things that could happen? If everything goes right, what are the best things that could happen? Then you can proceed with a confident realism.

Continue to meet regularly for worship, mutual support, discussion of successes, problems, failures, and resources.

12

A Reconciling People

The Christian has no alternative but to choose the way of reconciliation, which is also the way of self-giving, self-sacrificing, and suffering love.[1]

H is body beaten and bloodied, limp with pain and exhaustion. His head bowed with grief and pain and the weight of the world. Blood, mingled with the soldiers' spit, streaming from where the thorns and the nails pierced him. Men gambling for his clothes at his feet. Yet all this pain, this grief, and this weight could not dull his compassion. Indeed, it flowed forth all the more. Our Lord Jesus Christ dying on the cross for *our* sins.

In the temple, not far away, the finely embroidered, heavy linen veil separated the holy place from the holy of holies. Only once a year could a human being enter the holy of holies, and then only with an offering of blood to atone for the sins of the priest and of the people. Suddenly, the unsettling sound of tearing cloth set the temple abuzz. The veil had been torn in two, from top to bottom, as Jesus slumped dead on the cross! *His* blood had broken the barrier between God and humans. Jesus, our mediator, had given us access to God.

His friends were distraught, his enemies overjoyed. Jesus was bound up in white linen and tucked away in a little cave behind a huge rock with soldiers standing guard. So much for his messianic pretensions. Maybe the fishermen would all go back to their nets now. This disturbing episode had finally come to a close.

Or had it? The huge rock had been moved without human touch. The grave was empty, except for the burial linen laid neatly aside. The angel told his followers that he had risen! Jesus had won the victory over sin and death. He lives!

The crucified Christ, the risen Lord, Jesus as mediator between God and humans. The writers of the Old Testament had anticipated these events. They had experienced God's redeeming grace through the sacrificial system which had to be repeated year after year; yet they looked forward to the coming of the Messiah who would fully and finally reconcile them with God.

Jesus fulfilled their hopes and their prophecies. In his words and deeds, he proclaimed the Good News that he fulfilled in his death and resurrection. Jesus' self-giving sacrifice and victorious return to life are the central focus of the New Testament. We who build our lives on Christ also find them to be the central focus of our faith. We treasure every word and every deed of Christ that Scripture records; yet when we consider who we are and why we are here, we must forever return to these critical events. As the body of Christ, we must be engaged in following Christ's example. As Paul said, "I want to know Christ and the power of his resurrection and the fellowship of sharing in his sufferings, becoming like him in his death, and so, somehow, to attain to the resurrection from the dead" (Philippians 3:10-11).

Paul knew that following the example of Christ would set us apart from the ways of the secular world. "For the message of the cross is foolishness to those who are perishing, but to us who are being saved it is the power of God," he wrote (1 Corinthians 1:18). We are called-out people. We live according to God's wisdom, not human wisdom, and we follow the example of Christ, not that of our peers.

This difference shows itself not only in acts of personal devotion, such as Bible-reading and prayer, but in our every interaction with fellow human beings. God has called us to continue Christ's work as a reconciling people. As Lyle Schaller put it, "The Christian is called to act in a spirit of love, mercy, and charity to both friend and foe, to both supporter and opponent, to both the oppressed and the oppressor." [2]

This comes as a real challenge as we involve ourselves in various types of social ministry. It is relatively easy to carry a Bible to church and to be caring toward our friends and fellow Christians. Biblical virtues seem harder to practice when we deal with people who "aren't like us," who oppose practices from which we or our friends benefit, who are perpetually needy, who hold power but wield it unjustly, who oppose our efforts for social justice, or who accept the fruit of our labor but give no thanks.

In such instances the images of Christ illumine and stimulate our faith. We experience in a deeper way the compassion of Christ, whose love for the unlovely took him to the suffering of the cross. We must ask him to love others through us. We are humbled by the righteousness of Christ, which makes him a worthy mediator between humans and God. We depend upon him to intercede for us and to strengthen us. Finally, we are given hope through the power of Christ, who could not be held by death. He rose to raise up also those who believe and submit to his Lordship. As we die to ourselves in daily service to Christ, he fills us with his life everlasting.

Thus as we experience the reconciliation of Christ, we ourselves act as reconciling people. His grace grows in us as we reach out in grace to others. We can't outgive God—not in time, in money, in energy, in service, or in grace.

From the examples of Christ's ministry recorded in the Four Gospels we can learn some very contemporary lessons about possible pitfalls and strains in social ministry.

Ten men, their skin white with the living death of leprosy, awaited Jesus' approach and called out imploringly, "Jesus, Master, have pity on us!" He saw their need and responded with compassion. "Go show yourselves to the priests," he told them, for the priests had to verify that one's leprosy had been cured before one could return to normal life. They hurried off in excitement, for even as they went they found themselves healed. Only one man, a Samaritan, turned around and ran back to thank Jesus. Jesus did not hide his disappointment that only one of the ten had thought to thank and praise God (Luke 17:11-19).

This incident ought to prepare us with a healthy realism. There will be times when we will give and give and give some more but receive no thanks for what we do. We will be tempted to feel snubbed, to become bitter, and to determine to give no more. The example of Christ, however, compels us to compassion. Christ could have said, "That's it! No more healing for me! Only 10 percent glorified the Father as a result of my efforts—that's a very poor return. Just not worth it. You can forget the cross. Why should I give my *life* when people don't even appreciate my healing?" But no, Christ did not react in that way. He expressed disappointment at the men's ingratitude, but their ingratitude did not cancel out the worth of what he had done. He picked up and went on healing and teaching, confident that God sees and rewards when humans do not.

Discouragement and despair are two of Satan's most effective weapons. He uses them deftly to deaden enthusiasm, commitment, and hope, especially when situations seem weighted against us. There will be times when we must seek justice from people who think only in terms of their own interests or profit. That we might really achieve justice seems the *least* probable of all possible outcomes, and Satan would have us think only in terms of the *most* probable. He would turn our hope into pessimism, our enthusiasm into cynicism, our commitment into dust.

But faith does not concern itself with probabilities; it concerns itself with the power of God. Jesus told a parable that encourages us to persist in faith and prayer, the parable of the persistent widow and the unjust judge (Luke 18:1-8a). The judge did not fear God or care about humans. He certainly didn't care about the widow who kept coming to him seeking justice against an adversary. Widows were among the least powerful people in that day. Why should he concern himself with her cause? Yet she persisted in coming to him with her plea, so that finally he gave in, saying, "Even though I don't fear God or care about [people], yet because this widow keeps bothering me I will see that she gets justice, so that she won't eventually wear me out with her coming!" Jesus closed the parable with the words, "Listen to what the unjust judge says. And will not God bring about justice for his chosen ones, who cry out to him day and night? Will he keep putting them off? I tell you, he will see that they get justice, and quickly."

Many people of good intention have reached out to help others but have ended up offending them. Why? Because they offered their help in a paternalistic spirit. "My, my, you *certainly do* need help, don't you? Well, look, out of the goodness of my heart I am reaching out a helping hand to you so that you can better yourself. Just make sure you do it according to *my* terms." Of course, no one would actually say these things, but the attitude comes across nonetheless. And no wonder those being "helped" take offense.

Contrast the paternalistic attitude with the example of Jesus. During the last supper, Jesus wrapped a towel around his waist, filled a basin with water, and washed his disciples' feet, even those of his betrayer, Judas Iscariot. It is this spirit of servanthood that Paul exhorts us to follow.

Your attitude should be the same as that of Christ Jesus:

> Who, being in very nature God,
>   did not consider equality with God something to be grasped,
> but made himself nothing,
>   taking the very nature of a servant,
>   being made in human likeness.
> And being found in appearance as a man,
>   he humbled himself
>   and became obedient to death—even death on a cross!
>   —Philippians 2:5-8

If the Son of God did not exhibit paternalism, neither should we.

Being a servant does not mean being weak or wishy-washy. Witness the zeal with which Jesus cleansed the temple of the corrupt money changers and merchants. Mark Hatfield has commented upon this episode:

> The compassion of Christ could not simply co-exist with injustice; it embodied God's justice and righteousness, and unavoidably clashed with the corporate sin of the world. That clash culminated in the victory of the cross and the resurrection.[3]

We see the full quality of Christ's servanthood in the garden of Gethsemane as he uttered the words, ". . . yet not my will, but yours be done" (Luke 22:42). The agony of the cross haunted him—the agony that he, the sinless One, should take the sin of the world upon himself and endure separation from God. He asked to be spared, if only God were willing. Yet his submission completed the task of his compassion, "Not my will, but yours be done."

Seeing this submission in Christ, we ought to refrain from the pitfall of being too adamant in our own agendas. We may feel they are very well-conceived, and of course they are well-intentioned; but have we laid our plans before the Lord for his guidance? Submission often means sacrifice, but the servant acknowledges that the Master knows best.

There are times in social ministry when loving one's enemies sounds like a tall order. How can you love a perpetrator of injustice? How can you love someone whose actions hurt other people? How can you love someone who stands in the way of healing and wholeness for people? How can you love someone who resists attempts to be helped? How? By remembering that Jesus died on the cross for them. Jesus, who said, "Father, forgive them, for they do not know what they are doing" (Luke 23:34). How can we dare *not* to love them?

Lyle Schaller has illustrated how our love for friend and foe must be present in our social action, even in strategic noncooperation.

> In this spirit the churchman who marches on a picket line not only is witnessing to his concern for the oppressed, he also is suffering with those against whom he is protesting. He marches in a spirit of protest, but also in a spirit of reconciliation. He marches knowing that he is protesting the actions of a sinful man in a sinful world, but also knowing that he too is a sinner in need of God's forgiving and redemptive love.[4]

There will be times when Satan will throw obstacles in the way of planned action. Someone's cooperative *yes* suddenly becomes *no*. A blinding blizzard hits on the day of an important rally. A vital source of funds dries up. Key leaders in your social ministry are co-opted by those who have tried to discourage your work. Such hindrances should come as no surprise. Satan has a vested interest in impeding the Lord's work. Just as the disciples, however, turned from the obstacle of the cross to the miracle of the empty tomb, we should turn from despair to hope. Satan's obstacles become God's opportunities. Our part is to pray and to persist in faith.

Speed Leas and Paul Kittlaus give a good example of how Christians, as a reconciling people, can turn a negative situation into a growth experience.

> The police department in a city south of Los Angeles had received a large amount of bad publicity from a reporter who heard a lieutenant give a speech to local merchants on how to identify and deal with potential shoplifters. The officer's racist remarks and suggestions for dealing with minorities were shocking to many in the community. Instead of joining picket lines in front of the police station, however, the interdenominational ministry with which we were working offered its services to help train police personnel and generally raise the consciousness of the entire force. Rather than join the attack, we offered help. Our offer of services was accepted and the church agency collaborated with the police department in helping to change the behavior and attitude of its employees. Called into play were ministries not only of reconciliation, but also of healing, sustaining, and guiding.[5]

In other cases, being a reconciling people means helping people develop their own parallel power structures so that they can deal as equals with those who would oppress them. Voice of Calvary's ministry of cooperative ventures illustrates this. Having their own cooperative store, farm supply outlet, medical clinic, and housing not only helps to supply basic needs but also has reduced the economic dependency of the black population on the white population. It has increased their power and their ability to participate as equals in society.

GLEAM (Greater Lawrence Ecumenical Area Ministry) in Lawrence, Massachusetts, provides another example of God's reconciling people at work. This ministry has helped to organize a low-income neighborhood to stop the process of deterioration and promote revitalization. The ministry initiated services such as day care and tutoring while simultaneously working to get the neighborhood together, providing a forum for the people to take leadership in improving their area. Spiritual revitalization has been an integral part of the process, and the neighborhood has sprouted with hope and life.

The examples could go on and on. So could the needs. And so must God's people. Before we close this chapter, however, let us focus in on one more image from Scripture which is vital to our task.

The disciples had gathered together on the day of Pentecost. No doubt they were discussing all that had happened since Jesus' resurrection and his ascension into heaven. Suddenly they heard a sound like a strong wind blowing through the entire house where they were. Then they saw what looked like tongues of fire; the fire separated and rested upon each one of them, and they were filled with the Holy Spirit. Thus were Jesus' words fulfilled, "you will receive power when the Holy Spirit comes on you; and you will be my witnesses in Jerusalem, and in Judea and Samaria, and to the ends of the earth" (Acts 1:8).

We are God's people, called for a purpose. Let us go forth, then, not in our own power, but in the power of God's Spirit.

ENGAGE

Practicing Your Part

What do making a long-distance phone call and taking part in a role play have in common? They are both "almost like being there." In a role play you try to enact a specific situation, making it as true-to-life as possible. You step into a character's shoes—they may even be your own—and attempt to see and experience life from that person's perspective, acting and reacting in the situation as that person might. In the process you gain an understanding of the dynamics of the situation, the forces pushing and pulling the various people involved; you have an opportunity to try out various approaches to a touchy situation; and in those role plays in which you play yourself in a particular situation, you have a chance to hone certain skills, to learn how you react, and to evaluate your strengths and weaknesses.

Role Play 1: Refer back to minicase 2 on page 141 for the background for this role play. The scenario for the role play is a special, social-action-committee meeting called after the chairperson, Russ Johnson, has received the phone call from Sally Randolph, the store manager and member of ABC church. Peter Stambaugh, Nancy DeVries, Phil Milanowski, and Sara Martinez are the other members of the social-action committee. Sara, the daughter of migrant farm workers, brought the boycott to the attention of the committee and suggested that they become involved. Peter vigorously supported the idea. Nancy went along with it without expressing any real opinion. Phil also went along with it but expressed a few reservations that it might arouse conflict within the congregation.

Choose members of your group to play each of these committee members, as well as Sally Randolph; Bill Murray, the United Farm Workers representative; and Reverend Howard, pastor of ABC church.

The latter three people have been invited to join the meeting ten minutes after the social-action committee has initially met.

Russ Johnson begins the meeting with prayer, then tells the committee about the phone call he received from Sally. . . . (Carry on, identifying with your character as closely as possible and dealing with the situation as he or she might.* Continue the role play until the various points of view have been sufficiently expressed so that the group experiences the tension of the situation—whether or not the group arrives at a conclusion—or for a maximum time of twenty minutes.)

Evaluation:

1. To what extent were you able to identify with your character and realistically play his or her role?

2. How did taking part in (or watching) the role play help clarify the issues, points of conflict, and alternative resolutions for you?

3. To what extent do you feel that taking part in the role play helped you to develop skills in discussion, decision making, and conflict resolution?

4. Do you feel that role playing could help you to develop your skills and prepare to meet and deal with specific "tough situations" that may arise as you act to attain your group goals and fulfill your purpose?

Role Play 2—It is hoped that you answered yes to the last question because helping your group to function effectively in your task is what this role play is all about. Choose a "tough situation" that you (as a whole group, or that one or some of you) have encountered or anticipate. It should be a representative situation that the whole group can benefit from participating in or observing. For instance, if your group will be petitioning the local electric company for lower rates, those who will be visiting a representative of the company should play themselves; another group member should play the electric company's representative; and the rest of the group should observe, critique what goes on, and offer constructive feedback after the role play in order to help those visiting the company to carry out their task more effectively. (Remember that role playing, like the "real thing," involves risk, so offer your feedback in an upbuilding manner. As you evaluate, keep in mind some of the pitfalls and strains dealt with in this chapter.)

*If you have more group members than there are characters in the role play, they should observe silently in order to take part in evaluating the role play afterwards. If you have fewer members than there are characters, eliminate some or all of the last three characters.

Evaluation:

Post-role-play feedback should touch upon the following:

1. Did the role play situation seem as realistic as possible?
2. How might the situation be changed if one or more of the characters were to act/react differently? (How prepared are your group members for dealing with the different alternatives?)
3. What actions/reactions of group members that came out in the role play could be altered or improved in order to achieve group goals better?
4. Do group members need to develop specific skills in order to carry out their tasks better? If so, what skills, and how might they be developed?

Role play is an excellent tool that your group could regularly use for skill building, problem solving, heightening awareness, dissipating anxiety, and preparing for tough situations. It could also help you deal with tensions that might arise within your group. If group members are experiencing conflict that they find difficult to resolve, they might role-play a typical conflict-arousing situation but switch identities so that they can see the situation from the other persons' perspectives and also see how they themselves are perceived. One person not involved in the conflict should act as a "referee" in this type of situation. The referee should make sure that the role play keeps on a constructive track, should call "time" when the issues have been sufficiently explored, and should lead an evaluation discussion aimed at achieving mutual understanding and reconciliation. The goal is to heighten your sensitivity for the other persons' viewpoints and feelings and to foster communication.

How's It Going?

As you carry out your strategy, you should constantly evaluate your progress, your effectiveness, the appropriateness of your strategy, and the level of your group's cohesion and commitment. It makes no sense to develop a strategy and then stick rigidly to it when other important variables might be changing. Perhaps new facts have come to light that make a certain step unnecessary or inadvisable. Perhaps your timeline proves unrealistic, and you take longer to do a good job on certain steps than your planners anticipated. Perhaps group members are becoming discouraged because they feel too rushed, or too bored, or lacking in skills; if the strategy and timeline remain unchanged in light of such discouragement, commitment might fall off until one or two people are left holding the reins.

For this reason, it is vital to evaluate every action taken, as a group or within the subgroups responsible for a particular step.

Harry Fagan in his book *Empowerment* suggests using the following questions in the evaluation process:

1. What was the outcome?
   a) Was the action goal achieved?
   b) If not, why not?
   c) What were the social changes achieved?
   d) How much was due to the group's actions, and how much was due to other factors?

2. What about the anticipated group effects?
   a) Did the group members develop their skills?
   b) Did the group strengthen itself internally?
   c) Is the group now taken more seriously by others?

3. Were there any unanticipated side effects?

4. Were the outcomes (action goal achievement and side effects) worth the efforts, energy, time and resources expended? If not, what was changed?

5. Did the group follow the method specified in the plan? If not, what was changed?

6. Were there delays in meeting deadlines? Were delays due to the group's inefficiency or to outside factors?

7. What problems came up in any of the process or outcome components?[6]

This evaluation process will help you address your issue more efficiently, in terms of the effectiveness of your strategy and the use of your group's energy. Part of the evaluation process involves deciding what minimum measures of success your group is willing to achieve and still keep going—success in terms of meeting your goals and success in terms of development of your group and of individual group members. It also involves deciding whether you have satisfactorily met your goals and fulfilled your purpose. The group must then determine how to maintain the progress you have achieved and whether to disband or to continue as an action group.

Keeping on Keeping on—Resources

As you work toward your goals and as you seek to grow in skill and knowledge, you may find some of the following resources to be helpful.

Dale, Duane D., *How to Make Citizen Involvement Work: Strategies for Developing Clout;* and Speeter, Greg, *Power: A Repossession Manual—Organizing Strategies for Citizens,* both published by the University of Massachusetts Citizen Involvement Training Project. Amherst, Mass.: University of Massachusetts Press, 1978.

Both of these manuals are focused to promote and develop citizen involvement in public decision making. They provide analyses of various types of action that may be taken; describe how to obtain and wield power for your cause; and give practical, step-by-step guidelines for organizing an action group and taking effective action. Their particular focus is neighborhood or community organization.

Fagan, Harry, *Empowerment: Skills for Parish Social Action.* New York: Paulist Press, 1979.

This manual covers much of the same ground as Dale and Speeter but does so from the perspective of parish or church group involvement. Hence it provides a Christian perspective on motivations for social action and discusses the role of the Christian faith in one's attitude and conduct throughout the action process.

Leas, Speed, and Kittlaus, Paul, *The Pastoral Counselor in Social Action.* Edited by Howard J. Clinebell and Howard W. Stone. Philadelphia: Fortress Press, 1981.

This book explores ways of getting people involved in a social-action group, processes for helping people become more competent in social action, and methods for dealing with blocks that may arise in social-action groups. It features a unique blend of the pastoral care and social-action perspectives, so that persons, group dynamics, and action goals are covered as interdependent, interacting entities.

Pinson, William M., *Applying the Gospel: Suggestions for Christian Social Action in the Local Church.* Nashville: Broadman Press, 1975.

This book provides an apologetic for church involvement in Christian social action, then gives practical guidelines for moving to action. It has helpful chapters featuring practical suggestions for church social action, examples of church involvement and resources.

Schaller, Lyle E., *The Change Agent: The Strategy of Innovative Leadership.* Nashville: Abingdon, 1972.

This book explores the nature of social change and how to bring about planned change. It sketches different styles of leadership in the change process, describes the use of power in social change, and examines ways to anticipate and manage conflict. Written from a Christian perspective, it includes in its study the role of and the effects of change upon the institutional church.

Schultejann, Marie, *Ministry of Service: A Manual for Social Involvement*. New York: Paulist Press, 1976.

This book outlines a theology of Christian service and provides guidelines for developing a successfully sustained social ministry. It has practical suggestions for involving persons, training them for service, and supporting them in their tasks so that they find meaning and fulfillment. Approximately two-thirds of the book is devoted to helpful, down-to-earth suggestions and resources for social ministry.

Notes

Chapter 1

[1]J. R. Tolkien, *The Two Towers,* (New York: Ballantine Books, 1965), p. 171. Published in England by George Allen & Unwin, Publishers, Ltd. and used by their permission.

[2]William Smit, "Primary and Secondary Groups," in *Christian Perspectives in Sociology,* Wm. Smit, ed. (Grand Rapids: Calvin College Sociology Dept., 1980), pp. 36-37.

Chapter 2

[1]C. S. Lewis, *The Best of C. S. Lewis* (Grand Rapids: Baker Book House, Canon Press, 1969), p. 435.

[2]For further study see C. F. Keil, *Commentary on the Old Testament,* Volume 9, *Ezekiel–Daniel,* trans. James Martin (Grand Rapids: Wm. B. Eerdmans Publishing Co., reprint, 1973), pp. 351ff.

[3]Also Exodus 22:21; 23:9; Leviticus 19:33; Deuteronomy 10:18-19; 15:14-15.

[4]Speed Leas and Paul Kittlaus, *The Pastoral Counselor in Social Action,* ed. Howard J. Clinebell and Howard W. Stone (Philadelphia: Fortress Press, 1981), pp. 17-25.

Chapter 3

[1]Paul Ramsey, *Basic Christian Ethics* (New York: Charles Scribner's Sons n.d.), pp. 243, 347.

[2]Stephen Mott, *Christian Social Action Lectures* (So. Hamilton, Mass.: Gordon-Conwell Theological Seminary, 1980), p. 391.

Chapter 4

[1]Stephen C. Mott, *Biblical Ethics and Social Change* (New York: Oxford University Press, 1982), pp. 79-80.

Chapter 5

[1]Mike Barnicle, "The Meanest Corner," *Boston Globe* (March 4, 1981).

[2]Stephen C. Mott, *Biblical Ethics and Social Change* (New York: Oxford University Press, 1982), pp. 82-83.

Chapter 6

[1]Richard Collier, *The General Next to God* (New York: Elsevier-Dutton Publishing Co., Inc., E. P. Dutton, 1965), pp. 21-26.

158   A PASSION FOR JESUS; A PASSION FOR JUSTICE

Sallie Chesham, *Born to Battle* (New York: Rand McNally and Co., 1965), pp. 9-10.
Collier, pp. 174-5.
Ibid., pp. 175-6, 185-6.
Ibid., pp. 194-6.
Ibid., pp. 121-45.
William Booth, *In Darkest England and the Way Out* (London: International Headquarters of the Salvation Army, n.d.), pp. 233, 256.
Ibid., p. 36.
D. James Kennedy and Archie B. Parrish, *Evangelism Explosion*, rev. ed. (Wheaton, Ill.: Tyndale House Publishers, 1977), p. 200.
John M. Perkins, *Let Justice Roll Down* (Glendale, Calif.: G. L. Publications, Regal Book, 1976), p. 219. Used by permission.
Ibid., p. 109.
Ibid., p. 222.
Dennis E. Shoemaker, *The Global Connection: Local Action for World Justice* (New York: Friendship Press, 1977), pp. 4-5, 97. Used by permission.

Chapter 7

David Watson, *I Believe in the Church* (Grand Rapids: Wm. B. Eerdmans Publishing Co., 1978), p. 163.
Bruce C. Birch and Larry L. Rasmussen, *Bible and Ethics in the Christian Life* (Minneapolis: Augsburg Publishing House, 1976), pp. 42-43. Reprinted by permission.

Chapter 8

Richard J. Mouw, *Political Evangelism* (Grand Rapids: W. B. Eerdmans Publishing Co., 1973), p. 55.
Mark Hatfield, *Between a Rock and a Hard Place* (Waco, Tex.: Word Inc., 1976), p. 27. Used by permission of Word Books, Publisher, Waco, Texas 76796.
Harvey Cox, *The Secular City* (New York: Macmillan, 1965), pp. 140-141, 143.
For further analysis, see Robert Webber, *The Moral Majority: Right or Wrong?* (Westchester, Ill.: Good News Publishers, Cornerstone Books, 1981).
Patrick Devlin, *The Enforcement of Morals* (London: Oxford University Press, 1965), pp. 23, 25.
Hatfield, p. 217.
"Congressional Voting Record on Hunger-Related Issues, 1981," Bread for the World publication.
"Congressional Voting Record on Hunger-Related Issues, 1981."
"Finding the Energy to Continue," *Christianity Today*, 24:20-4 (February 8, 1980).

Chapter 9

Howard P. Jones, "Citizen Groups, Tool of Democracy," *Annals of American Academy of Political and Social Science* 199, (September, 1938), p. 176.
"Voter Turnout," America, 143:323 (November 22, 1980).
Richard J. Mouw, *Political Evangelism* (Grand Rapids: Wm. B. Eerdmans Publishing Co., 1973), p. 55.
John B. Wood, "Up Against Industry and the Budworm," *New England Magazine, Boston Sunday Globe* (April 25, 1976), p. 34.

Chapter 10

"A Guide to Effective Letter-Writing on Hunger Issues," published by Bread for the World, 6411 Chillum Place N.W., Washington, DC 20012; and "How to Write an Effective Letter to Your Congressperson" and "Visiting Your Congressperson," published by Network, 806 Rhode Island Avenue, N. E., Washington, DC 20018.

2"A Guide to Effective Letter-Writing on Hunger Issues," Bread For the World publication.

3"Getting on the News," a Bread for the World publication. Guidelines are also available from Environmental Action, 1346 Connecticut Ave., NW, Washington, DC 20036, and from Media Access Project, 1609 Connecticut Ave., NW, Washington, DC 20009

Chapter 11

1Stephen C. Mott, *Biblical Ethics and Social Change* (New York: Oxford University Press 1982), p. 145.

2In urging slaves to remain obedient to their masters, Paul is not making a case for the justness of the system of slavery. Rather, he is opposing their quest for release from social obligations in the name of Christian freedom.

Some people have used Paul's admonitions to slaves here and elsewhere as an argument against Christians seeking social justice. This is an invalid argument, since Paul never addresses the matter of slavery in terms of its justice or injustice. This does not stem from opposition on his part to struggles for justice, but rather is something he holds in common with all other writers of his time.

For further study on this issue, see S. Scott Bartchy, *First Century Slavery and the Interpretation of 1 Corinthians 7:21* (Missoula, Mont.: Council on the Study of Religion Society of Biblical Literature Dissertation Series 11, 1973), pp. 299-300.

3William G. McLoughlin, "Civil Disobedience and Evangelism Among Missionaries to the Cherokees, 1829-1839," *Journal of Presbyterian History* 51 (1973), pp. 118-25, 139.

Chapter 12

1Lyle E. Schaller, *Community Organization: Conflict and Reconciliation,* (Nashville: Abingdon, 1966), p. 131.

2*Ibid.,* p. 133.

3Mark Hatfield, *Between a Rock and a Hard Place* (Waco, Tex.: Word, Inc., 1976), p. 125. Used by permission of Word Books, Publisher, Waco, Texas 76796.

4Schaller, p. 132.

5Speed Leas and Paul Kittlaus, *The Pastoral Counselor in Social Action,* ed. Howard J. Clinebell and Howard W. Stone (Philadelphia: Fortress Press, 1981), p. 13. Used by permission.

6Harry Fagan, *Empowerment,* (New York: Paulist Press, 1979), pp. 59-60. © 1979 by Harry Fagan. Used by permission of Paulist Press.